FRIDAY NIGHT LIES

The Bishop Sycamore Story

FRIDAY NIGHT LIES

The Bishop Sycamore Story

Andrew King
and Ben Ferree

Library of Congress Cataloging-in-Publication Data available upon request.

This book is available in quantity at special discounts for your group or organization. For further information, contact:

Triumph Books LLC
814 North Franklin Street
Chicago, Illinois 60610
(312) 337-0747
www.triumphbooks.com

Printed in U.S.A.
ISBN: 978-1-63727-223-7
Design by Nord Compo

To Alexa, my rock and my best friend,
and The Dude, forever by my side.
—AK

To everyone who never stops talking
about things no one else cares about.
—BF

CONTENTS

PROLOGUE

On any given fall Friday across America, more than 7,000 high school football games are being played. Nearly a million teenage boys don the pads and helmets of their school colors, drawing millions of fans and generating millions of dollars in revenue. The sport is a juggernaut—the unchallenged king of Friday night. From frigid New England nights to sweltering Texas summers, high school football is one of the only truly ubiquitous traditions in the country. But above all else, high school football is a local pastime, as ingrained in its communities as the regional dialect. So when high school football airs on ESPN, the most valuable cable programmer in the country, it isn't to drive ratings. Games in these windows don't provide fodder for the next day's sports talk programming; the players involved aren't on fantasy teams and betting on the games is illegal.

On the afternoon of August 29, 2021, the mighty IMG Academy faced off against the Bishop Sycamore Centurions of Columbus, Ohio, a school that, on paper, appeared to have the makings of the next big thing. It boasted an extremely impressive schedule of opponents from all over the country, a major draw to promoters Paragon Marketing, who scheduled the game for ESPN. Its roster looked solid, especially for a school that was just a few years old. Ten days before, they had played Archbishop Hoban, a perennial juggernaut in the Ohio high school football scene. The school had high aspirations, and pitched its recruits that they could someday be a powerhouse just like their opponents, with a gleaming campus in Columbus. But Bishop Sycamore was no IMG Academy.

Based in Bradenton, Florida, IMG Academy describes itself as "the world's most prestigious sports, performance, and educational institution." Established in 1978, the school is perhaps the most well-known name in high school sports, churning out professional athletes at a nearly unmatched clip. They provide an education, but their calling card is the athletes who wear their jersey. In a five-season span between 2017 and 2021, their football team went a combined 42–3 and were crowned 2020 national champions. Bishop Sycamore was never expected to beat them.

In truth, most of these details were irrelevant to the nationally televised broadcast.

The game was part of the 2021 GEICO ESPN High School Football Kickoff, an annual showcase of schools from around the country. Airing games from Thursday through Sunday, the matchups serve as something of a football season kickoff for ESPN, filling the air in the last weekend before college football begins and the network fires up its NFL coverage. Games typically draw around 300,000 viewers, comparable to the lowest-rated programming of most weekends for the network. Even for IMG, the game was expected to be a tune-up for more challenging games to come, a chance for players to gain some experience.

But on the other sideline, the moment was much heavier, and head coach Roy Johnson couldn't help but feel the moment. Accustomed to the Friday night lights of small-town stadiums, Johnson coached that Sunday afternoon under the sunny skies above Canton, Ohio, just a two-hour drive from Columbus. The Rust Belt town of just 70,000 was no different from those small towns, but its stadium was. The 23,000-capacity Tom Benson Hall of Fame Stadium is imposing in its own right, dwarfing even IMG's professional quality 5,000-seat home. And just beyond its boundaries lies the Pro Football Hall of Fame, housing the history of America's most popular game. "It definitely feels different," Johnson said. "It's the NFL Hall of Fame field. I think the rest of the team felt like it was an honor to play there. I don't think anyone would deny that. Of course it's a big deal."

Senior defensive back and receiver Devante Jackson could feel it when the players were warming up, running routes and getting used to the stadium's turf. Players were arguing. Some weren't focused. As he put it, they weren't "straightening up." They weren't serious or focused. "It was like everybody was so shocked we were playing IMG, it was like everyone was in a state [championship] game they had never been to," he said. "They [were] acting too happy."

For most involved with the Bishop Sycamore program, that pregame moment would be the last time they would describe their demeanor as "too happy." A few hours later, the team left the field after a 58–0 loss in which ESPN's announcing crew apologized on-air for the game. Onlookers worried for player safety. Comically blown plays became jokes online. Reporters familiar with the high school recruiting scene struggled to understand who they were watching play. But the on-field embarrassment was just the beginning of a saga that would reignite a years-old controversy in Columbus. What came next would result in hundreds of thousands of dollars in legal battles, criminal charges, an official state investigation, and a media feeding frenzy that included actor Kevin Hart and NFL player and TV personality Michael Strahan. For one brief moment, the country was obsessed with Roy Johnson.

* * *

More than a year later, Johnson woke up before sunrise on November 5, 2022. In the dark of the morning, just before 5:00 AM, he opened Twitter and saw a post from a fellow early-riser who was commenting on a blowout high school football game. The tweet referenced "Bishop Sycamore 2.0." That annoyed Johnson, who replied with an image he had shared many times before. It was four screenshots of scoreboards featuring IMG Academy games that had become routs. In each, IMG won by at least 50 points. "It would be Bishop Sycamore 5.0," Johnson tweeted with the image. Half an hour later, he came across another tweet from the day before that referenced something that "reeks of Bishop Sycamore," which frustrated him. "Smells like paperwork?" he replied, attaching a photo of a document from the Ohio Department of Education explaining that Bishop Sycamore would "be listed as registered with the Ohio Department of Education for the 2020–2021 school year." The previous December, the ODE released a 79-page report explaining the ways Johnson and the Bishop Sycamore team had presented fraudulent information to obtain that document. But to Johnson, it proved him right. Bishop Sycamore *had* been a school. He kept searching. By the end of the day, he had tweeted the four IMG Academy scores at 27 different accounts. He had tweeted the ODE document 19 times.

At the top of his Twitter page, his biography read simply, "Taking Accountability and Changing."

It wasn't Johnson's first tweeting session. Coming to the defense of anything related to COF (Christians of Faith) Academy or Bishop Sycamore had become commonplace for him, largely due to the fact that, for the first autumn in years, he didn't have a football team to coach or a school to attempt to organize. The variety of legal cases he faced were at a standstill, and the documentary for which HBO had purchased the rights to his life story had yet to be released. He was no longer drowning in interview requests or avoiding an open bench warrant. He had time to do anything. But he was tweeting.

In reality, the collapse that led to his Twitter meltdown was years in the making, and the culmination of a variety of schemes designed to—depending on who you ask—make Johnson famous, create a new powerhouse football program, give second chances to disadvantaged youth, and groom the next generation of great athletes. But the entire project would be doomed before any football games could ever be played within weeks of its launch in 2018. So why was it still the focus of Johnson's life four years later? Even he isn't sure. "The thing people can't figure out about me is why I didn't just call it quits just then. Why didn't I just quit pushing? That's a whole other story."

1

I LOVE IT WHEN A PLAN COMES TOGETHER

Roy Johnson grew up in the Bronx as one of six children, with four sisters and a younger brother. As a kid, one of his favorite memories was watching *The A-Team*, a 1980s action-adventure series from NBC. In the show, a fictitious United States army unit was tried by court martial for a crime. The group is adamant that they are innocent, and spend the next five seasons avoiding capture as they attempt to prove the government wrong and restore their good names.

The show embraces going over the top. With melodrama, explosions, and unrealistic scenarios, *The A-Team* is, for all intents and purposes, a fantasy. But for Johnson, the show's overarching theme—a persecuted man striving relentlessly against a system that he perceives to be unjust—would serve as an analogue for the most pivotal years of his life.

"I watched it religiously. I even watch it now," he said. "One of the things that I loved about it is that they always had a plan, but something would always go wrong. Even though something would always go wrong, in the end they would end up beating the bad guys. Hannibal always said, 'I love it when a plan comes together' because it was ironic.

The plan never came together like the way he wanted. For me, it's the same thing. A lot of things that were said can just be proven to be false, and then people are going to have to make their judgements from there."

Decades later, Johnson would be called a con man, a liar, and worse. He would be wrapped up in a national scandal, wanted by police, and disavowed by his church. But what really annoyed him was the time a *New York Times* reporter knocked on his father's door. That interaction, however, made him ask the rare thoughtful question to his dad. As a child, did Roy always want to be the center of attention? "He said, 'I don't know if you wanted it, but you definitely got it. You were the firstborn son and everyone loved you.'"

Johnson's younger brother Matt moved away from the Bronx to attend college and try out for the football team at The Ohio State University. That move was an influential one for Johnson, who met Jay Richardson, fellow football player, through Matt. The pair became friends, and in addition to their friendship, Johnson and Richardson quickly became business partners as Richardson looked to expand his reach beyond an NFL contract and Johnson continued to hustle, attempting to find his niche.

By the early 2010s, Richardson had spent nearly half of his life in the spotlight. Born in Washington, D.C., Richardson spent two years living in Guam and three years in Virginia before settling in Dublin, Ohio, a Columbus suburb, with his mother, Deborah Johnson, a Buckeye fan who graduated from Ohio State, where she played rugby and graduated in 1979.

Richardson was a star athlete at Dublin Scioto High School, and made the easy choice to attend Ohio State, where he excelled as a defensive end. He showed enough talent to be drafted into the NFL by the Oakland Raiders, who selected him with the first pick in the fifth round. He would play a combined five seasons in the league (with another season on a practice squad). In one of those stretches, he was signed by the New York Jets on April 16, 2012, before being waived on August 31. But in that short time, he was around New York long enough to get an inkling of his business sense—and his connection to Johnson. An article in New York paper *Metro* profiled Richardson:

> The Jets knew that they were getting a five-technique defensive end when they brought Jay Richardson into the team's offseason activities and minicamp, what they didn't know was that they got an insurance broker as part of the deal.
>
> Cut by the Seahawks after the 2010 season, Richardson had all but given up his dreams and ambitions of playing in the NFL and had moved back to Columbus, Ohio, to focus on his insurance company. In 2007, Richardson, along

> with partners Roy Johnson and Sean Morrow, went from commodities trading to a focus on insurance "where we saw the potential to make real money." They created JR and Associates to become insurance brokers.

The story detailed how Richardson returned to his phone after practice to find eight missed calls and 10 emails waiting for him, many involving "business development." He called himself an entrepreneur who was putting in football work between 7:30 AM and 5:00 PM before working in his hotel for a few hours and then spending another couple of hours studying his playbook. The story notes that Richardson had to "rely on his business partners to keep him briefed and updated on the important issues of the day."

That work ethic is evident in the number of projects, businesses, and jobs that Richardson would take on, especially after his playing career ended in 2013. First, he started the Jay Richardson Foundation with his mother. The foundation was an organization with a relatively nebulous purpose, with messaging centered around youth and family. "It is NEVER TOO LATE to create the 'Team Family' that you want. It takes love, commitment, consistency, and time. Today is a good day to begin," read a quote attributed to Deborah Johnson on the foundation's website, which is deactivated. No social media posts have been made since 2019. He would also sign on to a variety of media gigs, including a recurring job with Columbus TV station WSYX ABC6/FOX28, where he serves as an Ohio State football analyst. In 2021, he joined *The Reality Check* podcast, co-hosting the show with former Ohio State running back Maurice Clarett.

The duo of Johnson and Richardson have a working relationship dating back to at least 2011, when the pair began selling life insurance together in Ohio. And in a method that mirrored the paper trail of his football programs, Johnson's career as an insurance salesman involved lies, inaccuracies, and a failure to provide accurate information from the very beginning. According to Ohio Department of Insurance records, "on or about June of 2011 through April of 2013, Johnson submitted applications for insurance policies to American Heritage Life Insurance Company containing incorrect and/or false information."

Johnson's issues, however, wouldn't be discovered until 2018, when his license was revoked. In the report issued by the ODI at the time, they charged that Johnson submitted applications that contained "incorrect and/or false information," lied about never being terminated from a contract before, and failed to report being "terminated for any alleged misconduct."

Johnson was given the chance to attend a hearing and defend himself on the charges. He did not appear, and on June 5, 2018, his license was officially revoked.

Similarly, Richardson found himself with a rescinded license thanks to his outstanding debt. According to ODI records issued in August of 2014, Richardson had "outstanding tax lien judgements with the State of Ohio." Additionally, "on or about June 6, 2014, Richardson was issued a subpoena from the Department to appear for an interview. Richardson failed to appear for his interview as directed by the subpoena." Due to these two charges, Richardson's license was officially revoked on February 13, 2015.

But in late 2014, the pair moved away from insurance, instead filing a new business in Ohio called PCG Ohio LLC. The company's purpose was unclear, as was its name. And less than a year later, in November of 2015, the company changed its name to The Richard Allen Group, a reference to the church that the organization claimed to be connected to. The name itself alluded to the church and its founder, Richard Allen, a minister who was born into slavery and eventually started the African Methodist Episcopal Church in 1794, making it the first independent Black denomination in the United States.

For years, it was unclear what the Richard Allen Group was for or what it set out to do. But on June 23, 2017, a new company was formed with almost an identical name: The Richard Allen Group RE1 LLC. Once again formed by Johnson and Richardson, this iteration of the company added a new founding partner, Buffie Patterson. Weeks later, HER Realtors (touted on their website as the country's largest agent-owned real estate firm) announced a partnership with the Richard Allen Group. Their press release gives more detail into the companies' purported activities than any of their threadbare filings with the state:

> HER Realtors, central Ohio's largest independently owned and operated brokerage, today announced a partnership with The Richard Allen Group, the recently formed for-profit arm of the African Methodist Episcopal (AME) Church.
>
> Eden Regento Real Estate Consultants in Columbus, Ohio, merged operations with HER Realtors to spearhead this new partnership with The Richard Allen Group. "Our mutual goals are the economic redevelopment of our communities, job creation, and education on home ownership," said Buffie Patterson, former managing broker of Eden Regento. "We're excited to be involved with The Richard Allen Group and invest our time and resources in the communities of their church members."
>
> An HER community office is being established to handle the real estate needs of The Richard Allen Group and the AME Church members in the King Lincoln District of Columbus from which Patterson and other associates will work. Prior to that opening, a location is being scouted

for a second office in the Dayton area, with plans to open others across the state in the near future.

"Buffie Patterson and the seven other tenured Associates joining us from Eden Regento are top caliber agents whose professionalism and dedication are a great fit for our brokerage," said Louise Potter, senior regional vice president of HER Realtors. "They will continue to service the real estate needs of clients throughout central Ohio, in addition to members of the AME Church, but now with the enhanced support and exposure that HER Realtors can offer."

"Ohio communities are growing, and we are seeing new job development impact housing growth," said Sean Morrow, vice president of business development for HER Realtors. "This new partnership with The Richard Allen Group will enable us to deliver market expertise with expanded reach and resources for clients, while continuing to position ourselves and associates for new opportunities that are surfacing."

Much of the press release's language was the only public time that any details of The Richard Allen Group's activities were ever described or even discussed. But the phrase "for-profit arm of the AME Church" would be one that Johnson would return to. Throughout the next few years, it was the way he would describe his organization.

In September 2017, Patterson filed for a "foreign for-profit license" in Ohio, allowing a non-Ohio company to do business in the state. She represented herself as an employee of The VJR Group, a real estate company in Georgia. Her listed purpose was "professional consulting services, real estate, and advising." Johnson and Richardson would eventually change the name of the company to the Mjolnir Development Group in 2018, this time with the words "real estate" included in the "purpose" section of the filing. Lawsuits would eventually end the organization. The filing for the partnership between RAG and HER expired in 2022 after no one re-filed paperwork for the organization, which is required every five years.

By 2018, both Johnson and Richardson found themselves with revoked insurance licenses. But that didn't stop either man from participating in the scheme that would evolve into a football program. When Deryck Richardson—no relation to Jay—first met the duo, who he said he perceived to be "business partners," it was to discuss a plan to sell life insurance policies to the members of the AME Church in bulk. And, as far as he knew, AME officials were very aware. "The church was endorsing it."

In fact, Johnson claimed that the purpose of the insurance scheme wasn't to make money for himself or for Richardson, but to grow the wealth of the AME Church. He claimed the policies were sold to church members as a way to help fund the future and allow them to donate money posthumously rather than taking money directly out of their pockets. Johnson said in a 2019 interview that he, and sometimes Richardson, would go to church-related conferences and events several times a year and present the idea.

"The church's concern was economic development," Johnson said. "In economic development, you need some sort of endowment to support that, so the church wanted to get life insurance from members and pastors to leave for the Third District. We went to a couple different insurance companies and a couple different banks … and they approached us with that probably about 2015 or 2016, when it all started. We started researching how to get that all done. We would travel around to different conventions and churches with them and say, 'This is for economic development, which would leave behind an endowment for funds to help support real estate offices for economic development, provide jobs, help fund scholarships and schools, whatever they wanted to do.' The Bishop would make an announcement saying, 'Hey, we're doing this project here to help support economic development; we need you to fill out a form.' And we'd hand the forms out, people would fill out the forms and then you have people call and set up appointments and get information and put it together and then submit it to the insurance company or the bank.

"It's not like the policies get left to us or the Richard Allen Group or anything like that," he specified, claiming he doesn't know why the church ever turned against the idea. To him, it was an easy way to amass a large sum of funding. "If you have 50,000 members across the Fifth District and 1,000 of them get a $250,000 policy and leave it to the church, you now have an endowment of $250 million dollars that's just gaining interest and that you can use to do all the things you proclaim you want to do. I can understand if the policies were left to Roy Johnson, but the policies were never left to us. It doesn't make sense to leave it to us."

Columbus' AME Church Third District would later deny "any affiliation" with COF Academy or the Richard Allen Group, and accuse the school of "seeking donations" and contacting people about "life insurance" under their name.

Johnson is adamant that the church was involved from the beginning. In fact, he says church officials came up with the name. "If I was going to name something, I would have called it 'Roy's Shit!'" he exclaimed, laughing. Johnson forgets the fact that the company had already existed for a year with a different name. In fact, Johnson has started at least three different companies in Ohio that have had at least six names between them. Only one of those organizations did include his name: GMC Johnson and Associates LLC, a company he started in 2009. No public information exists on the company, except for a lawsuit against them and Richardson in 2012 claiming unpaid debts. Like most other court cases involving Johnson, it was dismissed when the court was unable to find Johnson or Richardson to serve them the subpoenas on the case.

To almost anyone who would become involved with the football scheme that came next from Johnson, the church's involvement was the biggest—and sometimes only—reason for their faith.

The AME Church is not only one of the oldest churches in the country, it's one of the largest. With more than 2 million members worldwide, it represents a major pillar of Black communities in America. With that reputation comes a sense of trust from those who are dealing with the AME Church or its representatives. "I grew up AME—my grandmother was a member of St. John's AME church in Cleveland for years, one of the oldest churches in Cleveland," said Ulysses Hall, who would become one of Johnson's coaches. "So I grew up AME and when you say 'AME Church' I'm like, 'Oh, okay.' That's kind of what drew my attention."

The church's uniquely extraordinary ties to the Black community also allowed its name to be used to engender good faith. To Hall, it indicated a "Black-owned" mentality that was a game-changer. But the size and scope of the church also made those familiar tread with caution. "It's the same in the Catholic church," Deryck Richardson said. "It's like that in any church. It's something that's just known—you don't attack the higher ups. You don't want to mess with the church."

To Deryck and others who have been around the church—and who have been part of Black communities in general—the life insurance plan wasn't a scheme that set off any alarms. In fact, it seemed to him that it was a way to close gaps in the kinds of insurance coverages that community members were often missing. "Specifically in the Black community, you have people who just don't buy life insurance on principle or because they don't see the value in it," he said. "They just think, 'Well, I'm going to die.' So we're underinsured as African Americans. What you find is that if you can have someone who endorses you, then you get a whole bunch of policies at once."

So the idea was to partner with the church, who could provide a captive and trusting audience, while giving that audience access to something they didn't already have. "You go to a church and the pastor says, 'Last week, Betty died and we had to pass the plate for her funeral. Here's an inexpensive option for you to allow people to provide for you so that the burden is taken off of the church and community and replaced with a $35 monthly bill,'" Deryck said. "We do that with churches and retirement homes rather than talking to them one-on-one."

But Johnson has a tendency to move through ideas quickly. And in what seemed like the blink of an eye to Deryck, what began as an insurance scheme would quickly morph into a plan to start a football program. It would be one of the more memorable experiences of his life.

2

THE IMG OF THE MIDWEST

Amid a sea of exaggerations, half-truths, and flat-out lies, one thing is certain: in February of 2018, there was a plan for COF Academy. The team made its debut on Twitter with an extremely dramatic hype video composed in the style of a movie trailer. "AME – New Salem presents," it begins, "the premier sports high school. Football. Basketball. Track. Soccer. Ironmen." Already, they had a name and they had a flair for the dramatic. The only text accompanying the video was a jubilant "We Here!!!!!"

At the time, Deryck Richardson had never heard of any of this. He entered the COF Academy orbit through his friend and business partner, Josh Harris, a central-Ohio native who played football at Bowling Green State University in northwest Ohio under Urban Meyer and would later coach at Ohio State. But Deryck wasn't part of the football world; he was a businessman. In late 2017, Harris introduced him to Jay Richardson (again, no relation) and Roy Johnson—he knew Jay from football circles, and only knew that Johnson was his longtime business partner. "As the story unfolded," he said, pausing to consider, "it was one of the most bizarre things I've been a part of."

Deryck's part in that saga began in his Columbus office, where Harris and Jay Richardson had set a meeting to discuss an insurance deal. The quartet's plan was to kill two birds with one stone: they'd advance their careers and earn some much-needed money by brokering an insurance agreement with the local district of the African Methodist Episcopal Church. The Richard Allen Group duo was adamant that leaders of the Third Episcopal District had cleared the project.

Regardless of how nebulous the ties between the scheme and the church were, Johnson was charismatic. Deryck found himself drawn to the man, though he knew very little about him. In fact, he saw himself in his new colleague. "Roy reminded me a lot of me. He thought outside the box, he was creative, he used his personality. Too often in business, people have a cookie-cutter vision of what it should be. Some of the best entrepreneurs are creative and think outside the box." He did not, however, have similar first impressions of Jay Richardson. "Jay was certainly not as outgoing as Roy. He was more standoffish. He was the type to say, 'Let's get to the point. I don't care how your kids are doing. I have things to do.'"

He recalled one instance—months after their introduction—where the group gathered at his office for a video shoot. While everyone else acted normally and respectfully, he always remembered that Jay Richardson "snuck out the back door" to avoid interacting with some of Deryck's employees, who were understandably excited about the prospects of an Ohio State and NFL player walking through their door. "I thought, 'That's kind of rude, bro.' We took the time to shoot a video for you and now you're running out of here like it's a bunch of groupies. It was just a few grown men saying, 'What's up?' That type of thing really shows your character, to me."

It didn't take long for Deryck to see just how far outside the box Johnson was thinking, and over the course of the next few weeks, as they planned the life insurance deal, Johnson's field of vision opened as he learned more about Deryck's qualifications. "As he would come to the office more and more," Deryck said, "he started saying, 'Wait a minute, you're an ex-teacher? You taught at a charter school, so you've seen the business side of schools being built?'" He also liked that Deryck had a background in marketing. In retrospect, those questions foreshadowed the shift that was beginning in Johnson's mind.

Eventually, Johnson began hinting at another project—he was planning on building a high school for the church. "I want you to come to this dinner," he told Deryck one day. "We're going to present our vision for this school, COF Academy." Johnson added one other small detail: his insurance license had been revoked. The school was now the plan. Without much information, Deryck attended the event. He was intrigued. But he was also alarmed by the fact that Johnson presented this pivot in such a matter-of-fact way. "What's fascinating is that the whole church project went from 'We're going to be able to present to the church and get some easy sales and take care of a community that's underinsured' to 'Let's work on this school' to 'Hey man, my [insurance] license is suspended so we can't do the church project anymore either.'"

* * *

On New Year's Eve of 2017, Ulysses Hall got a phone call from a number he didn't recognize. He let it go to voicemail, but the same number called back. Roy Johnson was calling. Hall had never heard of Johnson, but the voice told him that he was reaching out on the referral of Hall's friend, Paul Williams, who he knew from Ohio Wesleyan University, a small private school in central Ohio. Williams had signed on to be part of a new project, and Johnson started to sell Hall on the idea moments after he answered the phone. He told Hall that he "had an opportunity" for "a new endeavor" and asked him to send his résumé. Intrigued, Hall sent it over. The next day, he called Williams to ask who Roy Johnson was and whether he should be interested. "He said they were talking about making the IMG of the Midwest," Hall said. "That was literally the pitch."

A former college football player at Shaw University in North Carolina, Hall had a résumé that made him worth targeting for an emerging football program. He was serving as defensive line coach and assistant director of football operations at Wesleyan, and had previously coached a high school team in Georgia. He had come to Columbus to advance his career, and he understood coaching, recruiting, and specifically the world of Ohio football, all things Johnson needed help with. "I wanted to be a college ball coach," he said. "I was trying to do whatever I could to put myself in a position to be a coach at the highest level." Johnson told him his résumé was great. He said it was exactly what they were looking for in the new project he was working on. But Hall had a good job—he wasn't in a hurry to leave. And Johnson didn't inspire confidence in Hall early on. "I honestly didn't know [what to think]," he said. "He sounded like a guy trying to sell me." When Johnson brought up the AME Church connection, however, Hall's mentality shifted.

Hall grew up with a connection to the church through his grandmother, a member of St. John's African Methodist Episcopal Church in Cleveland, one of the oldest churches in the city. That connection instantly lent credibility to Johnson's plan. As Hall put it, "The opportunity was not only a school where we could play some ball and educate some kids, but a Black-owned school that they were trying to make a powerhouse. Those were the selling points: it was the church and it was Black-owned. I thought it was dope.... That conversation 100 percent goes differently if the church isn't part of the conversation. The church is what sold me in the first place. I'm like, 'Man, you can't go wrong with the church.'"

A few days later, Hall got an email from Johnson inviting him to an event at the AME Church in Columbus called "the Christians of Faith Academy Reveal." At the time, he was still unsure about whether he wanted to join the COF Academy staff. The move would represent a non-linear career path that he knew would be a risk. But there was no risk to attending an event, and he decided to go check it out.

That night, as he watched the presentation unfold on AME Church property, Deryck was impressed. Not only by what he saw, but by his company in the room full of 50 people. "The [Third District] Bishop is there, politicians are there, lawyers are there, big-time developers are there. They show us this rendering of a big facility and all the land they had. The whole thing was professional. There was food." Johnson was feeling good, too. "All of a sudden, a concept becomes a reality," he said with a smile in 2019. "Because now you have the support of people. You have these people who are affluent and can make things happen. You have a builder there who's built plenty of things around the country. You look at that and you're like, 'Man, these people really want to help.'" At one point, Johnson had to stop preparing for his speech and help coordinate the arrival of more food. There were too many mouths to feed. The night was already a rousing success.

In the same room, Hall was surprised by what he saw. He remembers seeing familiar faces from the football community, bankers, representatives from the Ohio Department of Education, AME Church leaders like Reverend Taylor Thompson and other pastors, even parents of professional athletes with church and Ohio ties. He chatted with developers about plans for the COF Academy infrastructure. Some men were wearing suits. Women wore dresses. There were refreshments. "This was, like, a real professional-seeming event." As the crowd quieted and a presentation began being displayed, the level of professionalism continued to climb.

"Please join us for the unveiling of COF ACADEMY on Monday, February 12, at 6:30 PM—112 Jefferson Ave Columbus," read a small flier that school leaders distributed in early 2018. Above the lettering, crudely drawn pictures of school supplies—a backpack, a protractor, a bottle of glue, an apple—made up the top half of the page. It was evocative not of a powerhouse football program or a tough bunch of castoff athletes, but of signage for a fourth-grade open house.

The digital version of COF Academy's early marketing was a stunning tonal shift. A presentation distributed by DVD offered a six-minute tour of the supposed future of the school. The video showcased an extensive, detailed rendering of what COF Academy was set to become. The first 40 seconds of the video were dedicated to the school's main campus. An aerial view showed hundreds of parking spaces, a long and visually striking building that wrapped around an impressive football facility encircled by a track, with an entire practice field on the other side.

On the back side of the football field and horseshoe-shaped building was a long pathway traversing a watery area that led to the school's living quarters. As a program that would pull talent from all over the country, the school needed somewhere for its students to live. The planned housing was impressive, with views that overlooked the water and sat next to a pair of baseball diamonds. State-of-the-art dorms were a major draw for many of the students COF Academy sought to attract. In fact, *any* dorms were a major draw. Many of the students who found themselves entangled with the program got there because of less-than-stellar living conditions back home. Many struggled with poverty. Some were living in states far from home. Several saw the school's promises as a way out of homelessness. The idea of living in a comped room with a view was attractive.

Johnson saw the plan as "a faith-based school that guides young men through life." Modeled after IMG Academy—but with a spiritual twist—the school could serve as a refuge, a launching pad and a stage for students who didn't have another way to reach their goals. "You do that through innovation of technology and sports and education and a place where you could come and be safe. And it's not just for the underprivileged kids, but also the kids who are good athletes from good homes. I believed that if you bring those kids in, it will help lift the other kids who are there." He would later claim that the plan was so much about the kids that he didn't even necessarily mean for it to be about football—that's just his world. "Sports was the easiest to do because I didn't know a band director. If I knew a band director, we would've worked in music, too," he said with a laugh.

The sky-high view of a massive, hypothetical facility fills less than two minutes of the more than six minutes of graphical representations of the school. The rest consists of close-up renderings featuring details like lobbies with vaulted ceilings, aesthetically pleasing walkways connecting points of interest, a playground for kids, murals on the outside of the facility, a team store, weight rooms, film rooms, and more. If all this detail seems out-of-character for a program now known for its haphazard execution, that's because it is.

The renderings and presentation were partially created by developer and attorney Mike Egan, a relative powerhouse in the world of sports development. Egan has been part of a number of major projects across the globe, including the Atlanta Olympics, Beijing Olympics, and sports facilities throughout America. At one point he owned and operated Sport Choice, a sports-focused development company based in California.

The morning before the big presentation, a collection of major players in the COF Academy project had gathered to talk details. The group included Johnson, Jay Richardson, Egan, Rev. Taylor Thompson, and other AME Church officials, representatives from multiple banks, and Jeff Kellam (owner of Indiana-based Kellam Inc.), who was brought in for construction expertise. Kellam, like others, had been pitched a philanthropic goal meant to improve the lives of students who would attend COF Academy. When he sat and listened to church and bank officials discuss finances, it only made him more confident in the plan. "I have a memory of the church representatives saying they were behind the project, and they said that to the banks," he said in 2019. "They were going to service the interim debt while they were raising donations and getting the money from the bank for what I'd call 'Phase 1.'" The pieces were falling into place.

For nearly everyone in attendance at the event later that night, the church's involvement was key. "There was a strategy to it all," Egan said. "It was clear that the AME Church said, 'We'd like to see you do this project without us putting hard cash into it up front. But you can use our resources, our finances, [to] leverage it and get things started.'"

Deryck agreed. "It certainly felt as if the church knew what they were doing. It's hard for me to believe that they pulled off having all these people coming to the meeting with all these renderings, and the church had no idea what they were doing."

At the beginning of the night, Hall was still undecided about his involvement in the program. He had been interviewing for college jobs, and didn't plan on taking what he perceived as a step backward into the high school ranks again. But the event changed his mind.

"I was still not sure, but that event helped me be even more on board because they showed us the blueprints for what they were trying to build. I mean, we saw this gigantic school; it was professionally done. [Plans] looked tremendous and it looked extremely expensive and legit. And then they talked about how they were going to the AME church and partnering with Mike's company and they were gonna build this and put up the money for it.... And they went down various game plans academically for the students—it wasn't supposed to just be for student athletes, but also I think it was for underprivileged students as well.

"At that point, I was all in."

Kellam left the presentation excited, too. With only about six months until football season began, he said the group was motivated and ready to move fast. With this kind of financial backing, the project could move quickly. He was happy to be involved. "We took off in a hurry," he said, "like a ball of fire." The timeline was challenging, but with AME backing, he thought it could be done. "There was no way that you could do a project of this size and not have a main supporter with deeper pockets—or at least deeper resources—to help organize and support it."

Even Egan, who has helmed enough projects to be able to spot signs of trouble, thought by that point that the project was coming together. "In a lot of ways, things happened exactly how they were supposed to," he said. "But as far as the issues toward the end, that's the part where I'm still scratching my head."

Depending on who you ask, those issues started developing over the months that followed the big reveal in the spring of 2018. Johnson thought he had secured his space, a seven-acre plot of land on Codet Road on the east side of Columbus. Situated near the massive Easton Town Center development, a sprawling outdoor/indoor mall surrounded by restaurants and other amenities, the location was shockingly prime real estate for a piece of land that was planned to be donated for free. Estimates set the value of the land near $7 million. It would be donated by New Salem Baptist Church, a congregation nearby. The group formed Codet Unity LLC through an attorney, and emails from New Salem Pastor Adam Troy say there were "no points of departure" from the plans that Egan and his team had assembled. Along the way, AME officials stayed involved. No representative from New Salem has ever returned calls for comment on a story involving COF Academy.

"I talked with people within the AME Church—administrators, staff, and everything—confirming the relationship between [the Richard Allen Group and the church]," Egan said. "And most of the time when we were having discussions about what we were going to do, I would say, 'Let's do this,' and Roy would stop me and say, 'Well, I have to go back and make sure it's okay with the church first.' It was always this guidance that was always there. I personally had face-to-face meetings with folks at the AME Church. It was all officials of the AME Third District."

That spring, Kellam and Egan hastily assembled a team that could complete the project. Egan said many of those he called worked for a "reduced price" because they "wanted to be supportive," and the first thing on the agenda was to clear the land that would become the shiny new school. The COF Academy pitch was a good one.

For Johnson, the first signs of trouble came in the form of the Indiana bat, a federally protected endangered species that nests in Ohio trees. Because of those protections, Ohio developers can't tear down trees containing the bats beginning in April. According to Johnson and Kellam, the proposed COF Academy land was riddled with bats. Construction was halted before it ever began.

Meanwhile, the likes of Egan and Kellam watched as the project became untethered from the church and it grew more and more challenging to track down a check. "The AME Church side of it just went away," Egan said. "They just started denying everything, which made no sense. All I could think was that there was some type of very big misunderstanding on their side. I didn't know if there was a vindictiveness; I didn't know if there was something else."

Kellam was less sympathetic. "My involvement ... stopped when I stopped being paid."

Back at his office, Deryck was having a similar experience. He had connected Johnson with Edmentum, an online academy he knew about from his days in education. He had helped with planning and guided Johnson on some of the strategies other schools had used to establish themselves. But with other businesses at hand and a rapidly decreasing faith in Johnson's ability to pay him, Deryck cut ties with Johnson and the Richard Allen Group. "We were paid in the beginning, and the check came from the Richard Allen Group, but pretty quickly, the money stopped. There were excuses about why there was no check, and I think we even had a check bounce."

Even then, however, he knew where he felt the problems began. "I've always put my blame on the church," he said. "I don't know what happened, but I do know that there was funding promised from the church and at some point they said no. I don't know how they said no. I don't know if they said, 'Shut down the school.' I don't know if they just pulled out. But at some point there was funding promised—and then there wasn't."

But seven months after the meeting at the church, with the team's football schedule underway, its Ohio Department of Education registration in doubt, and its leader running from a variety of legal cases, the AME Church's Third Episcopal District slipped a statement onto its website denying "any affiliation" with COF Academy or the Richard Allen Group. And in a twist that was particularly interesting to Deryck, the church called into question the group's original plans. "If persons come to you seeking donations to COF, please understand that the Third District has not authorized or condoned any person or entity to seek any donations in the name or authority of the Third District," the statement read. "If it is your desire to make a donation do so of your own free will with full knowledge that the Third District is not involved in any manner with either the COF or RAG or any of their activities."

The church's attorney, Arthur Harmon, doubled down on the statement days later. "The persons that were involved in this, I believe, may be AME members of a local church or something like that," he said. "But they have gone off into their own business enterprise and, naturally, wanted to present their business enterprise to the AME Church and its members to see if they would be interested in that. If there was any representation that there was an affiliation or that the AME Church or the Third District was approving or disapproving of any of their actions, then that's not the case. There is no affiliation."

Johnson didn't know how to feel. "Mad and disappointing, they hang out around the same line," he estimated in 2019. "I'm disappointed in the fact that a lot of kids were affected, and I'm hurt more than anything else. I'm also scared.... Naturally, you get upset and disappointed and they're all kind of the same. And you get angry because that's the natural way to lash out. I would've been disappointed if they had said, 'We don't want to do it.' But now they've denied us and lied and I'm mad."

Deryck was floored. "What I can definitely tell you is that they knew about it," he said. "I didn't like that they denied any knowledge of this. Something was there that made them deny it." When the news broke, Johnson turned off his phone and stopped doing interviews. But he didn't stop COF

Academy. "Roy had these connections, he had these kids, and he's already running down the hill when the church pulls out," Deryck said. "So he thinks if he stops, he'll fall apart, roll down the hill, and hurt himself."

3

HEY MAN, YOU'RE A GOOD-SIZED KID

While attempting to build a state-of-the-art high school campus and facilities for an elite sports program, a more pressing matter required attention: COF Academy needed to figure out how to get a football team on the field in a matter of months—and find a way to educate them.

By the spring of 2018, Roy Johnson had moved Ulysses Hall into a new apartment. "The church is handling all this stuff," he told Hall, which didn't seem far-fetched after sitting through a handful of meetings in which church officials discussed their involvement in the project. Although the massive development project churned in the background, that wasn't Hall's concern. He was there for football, and the new apartment and a fresh start felt like a way to emphasize just how committed he was to teaching young people to play the sport. "It was about coaching, recruiting, and handling football operations," he said. "I am a coach."

The team he would be coaching had a star-studded schedule packed with big-name programs, and Hall needed a team. He traveled the spring showcase circuit eyeing potential recruits for the school, but he wasn't looking for just anyone.

At the time, Johnson was largely leaving player recruitment up to the coaches. After discussing it, Hall and head coach Paul Williams had decided they were looking for players without catastrophic grade situations. They wanted players with GPAs of about 2.8—not Rhodes scholars, but not players they would need to worry about. Because if they needed to worry about some of the players keeping their grades up, they weren't sure the infrastructure would be in place to course correct. "We didn't want guys that were in too much academic, you know, trouble," Hall said. "We didn't think we would be equipped without knowing our full staff to handle that at the moment. So to be able to be sure they kept their grades up, that was the game plan. Kids with lower GPAs would require a little more help."

What they did know was that they would be working with a company called Edmentum and their EdOptions Academy program. Based in Minnesota, Edmentum is a company that specializes in "adaptive curriculum, assessments, and practice proven to improve student achievement" and provides online learning programs. Through EdOptions, they would develop the school's curriculum and provide software, a course catalog, and services to help administer the classes. At COF Academy's 2018 media day, consultant Melissa Rager said the programs were certified with the state of Ohio and the NCAA, and diplomas issued by Edmentum would function exactly like other Ohio diplomas. "We are considered an accredited institution; we're essentially a private school," she said. "Same with the NCAA, which is actually harder to do than the diploma piece. And that's why we're different—we're a diploma-granting institution. If students go to COF, they have the ability to go to the military, a four-year-school, a trade school." Hall, who had experience in a school, said he sent at least 50 emails back and forth to Edmentum. He trusted what they offered.

But while Edmentum may have functioned like a typical private school, COF Academy wouldn't. Johnson knew he had to register the program with the Ohio Department of Education, and he did so by taking advantage of a very specific part of the Ohio Revised Code. COF Academy would be classified as a non-chartered, non-tax-supported school, often known as an "08" school because of its inclusion in ORC Rule 3301-35-08. The designation exists for schools that are "not chartered or seeking a charter from the state board of education because of truly held religious beliefs." At 08 schools, parents are responsible for "reporting their child's school enrollment or withdrawal," and the ORC specifies that those in charge of the school "may, as a matter of convenience, provide" an attendance report. After specifying that teachers must have a bachelor degree, pupils must graduate between grades, and that the school must obey health and safety laws, legislation requires nothing else. No standardized tests are required of these schools and virtually no government oversight or interference is required. When registering with the state, Johnson ballparked an estimate that COF Academy would have 500 students.

At some juncture in the middle of 2018, Johnson and his team needed to decide whether to attempt to join the Ohio High School Athletic Association, the governing body of high school sports in the state. While there are a number of high schools and football programs throughout Ohio that do not join the OHSAA for a variety of reasons, not participating in the association and adhering to their rules means a program loses out on some perks. If a team is recognized by the OHSAA, be they a member of the organization or not, the OHSAA member teams they play will get points for victories. Those points accumulate throughout the season, and are used to determine which teams in Ohio make the playoffs each year. As part of Johnson's goal to be an easy opponent for elite programs, being able to count for OHSAA playoff points represented a major boost in helping the team develop a schedule each year. Johnson had also personally promised the schools he scheduled that they would get playoff points by beating them. As such, he still sought the smaller designation that came with being recognized but not a member school, which required far fewer checks than full membership. The only requirement was confirmation that COF Academy was, in fact, a school, along with verification of the total number of students enrolled in the school. It's that second requirement that became the loose thread that would unravel COF Academy.

Meanwhile, Hall and Williams were in a whirlwind of meetings. As they tried to find equipment for the season, they spent time with representatives from Adidas, who were feeling them out for an opportunity to get in on the ground floor of a big-name program. The duo worked to put together plans for how school and classes would function, settling on a method to "combine the academic schedule with the practice schedule." Hall felt good about what he had put in place, and was comforted by a sense of structure—finally. "It was laid out. They were going to practice from this time, lift from this time, [then] they were going to work. They were going to go to class for these hours on these days. I was told we really wanna do the IMG model, which is more like a college model where they'll practice in the morning, go to class for about five or six hours, and then, you know, have other practices, film, and all of that."

One of many steps that evaded COF Academy administrators' attention was the acquisition of proper licensure from the state of Ohio to even coach high school athletics. The ODE requires coaching permits "for individuals who will direct, supervise, or coach a student activity program that involves athletics, routine or regular physical activity, or activities with health and safety considerations." The permits are required by law, and are intended to help ensure that the people in charge of supervising minors in athletics have completed basic training. In addition to a nominal fee, applicants for the permits must complete five categories of training: Fundamentals of Coaching, CPR, First Aid, Concussion Training, and Sudden Cardiac Arrest Training. The process also includes a background check. None of Johnson, Hall, Williams, nor anyone else on the team ever applied for a permit. They would all go on to serve as head coach or assistant coach of the team at various stages, but none of them were legally eligible to do so.

At one point, Hall helped try to find a fit for a potential director of football operations position. He called Hudl, a company that provides technological assistance to football programs and makes connections between leaders. He told the person he spoke to that he was forming a new program, and they replied that they had heard there was going to be a new school and were excited to learn more. It was a good moment for Hall. For once, someone other than Roy was showing external excitement about the project he had been working on. "It wasn't like it was a secret. I'm saying that to help you understand just how legitimate we were under the impression everything was."

Hall kept plugging away, working on dozens of different projects at different times. Sometimes he was in charge of finding facilities for practices, film sessions, and other required amenities. At one point, he met with Lifetime Fitness near Easton Town Center, where he helped strike a deal that included a regional manager flying in from Minnesota. He found a strength and conditioning trainer to help with that aspect of the team and made plans for connected headsets and heart monitors to track player performance and organize workouts.

Sometimes, when he found recruits who were interested, Hall would bring them to Columbus to see the facilities. He told them about the plans to build apartments near Easton, which he conveyed were "getting finalized." Recruits stayed at the Baymont Inn in Delaware, just north of Columbus. In the background, Hall wasn't sure what was happening. That wasn't his role, and he didn't want it to be. "My job was football operations. The only thing I didn't handle in football operations was transportation." With a few months to prepare for the season, Hall and Williams were firm in their belief that no field was going to finish in time to host games. "We're going to be a road team," Hall and Williams settled between themselves, even while Johnson continued to present optimistic visions of an early field being completed in 2018.

The pair were incorrect, and the result of Johnson's optimism came in the form of a relatively new facility called Fortress Obetz, a 6,500-seat multi-use stadium which had opened in May 2017 in the village of Obetz, a small community south of Columbus. The site would serve as a home for three COF Academy games (and multiple practices) in 2018. However, a public records request filed with the village of Obetz yielded just one contract between Johnson and the village, which owns and operates the stadium, for a 14–12 loss to Dayton public school Dunbar. The cost to rent the facility was $1,750, but there are no documents showing that Johnson was billed for the other games that season, including their season opener against Football North. Obetz declined to answer whether that bill was ever paid.

But Fortress Obetz wasn't the first choice of home fields for Johnson; at least, it wasn't how he described COF Academy's home to the teams he was trying to schedule with. St. Ignatius, a perennial championship contender in Ohio, was the first program to add COF Academy to their schedule. In a statement posted on the school's website on February 12, 2018, they described the matchup with "COF Academy, the AMEC's first Non-Public, Non-Charter private school." The statement listed the time and date of the game, but admitted that the site was "to be announced." However, the statement also provided insight into the lofty goals Johnson was sharing with his prospective opponents. "Memorial Stadium at Otterbein University and Ohio Stadium on the campus of The Ohio State University are among the possible sites—and we emphasize, possible sites. Coach Urban Meyer's Buckeyes are at TCU the weekend of September 14th. COF Academy, which is expecting to welcome around 800 students for its inaugural year, has a 61-acre campus located in Columbus, Ohio, that will include innovative classrooms and athletic facilities. The school is preparing for 19 sports in its athletic program."

By late spring, the COF Academy coaching staff knew they weren't going to be able to field a team as large as they had hoped. Hall thought they could maybe reach 20 kids, but even that would require some effort. That's when Johnson began to influence player selection. "Roy wanted more guys of course, so I'm like, 'Well, Roy, I don't know what else to do at this point. We got who we have, let's work with who we have.'"

One day, Hall was chatting with Johnson about Kadeem Shabazz, a player he knew personally. The year before, Shabazz's father had died suddenly in the middle of his son's senior year of high school. For Shabazz, it was a lost season after spending his football time mourning the loss of his father. Having known both of them, Hall wished he could help. Johnson had an idea, telling Hall, "You know they have the option to reclass." That didn't mean much to Hall, but it introduced an idea to Johnson that would become a crucial piece of the foundation of COF Academy and Bishop Sycamore.

Shabazz reclassified, got his lost season back and played for COF Academy as a 19-year-old, which felt odd to Hall, though he knew it was for a good reason. "He was my one contribution, in terms of reclassed [players]. The rest of the kids that Paul and I had brought up were high school kids—either sophomores, juniors, or rising seniors in high school. Where it got crazy was when Roy was like, 'This isn't enough guys.'"

As part of his pitch to recruits, Johnson would often reference his desire to create a TV show around the school, particularly modeling the idea after the documentary series *Last Chance U*, a Netflix production that follows the lives of student-athletes at junior colleges. In the show, players are chasing their perceived "last chance" at a career in sports by attending a junior college in an attempt to make an impression on a Division I university. Johnson had the same idea—but for post-grads continuing to play high school football.

To anyone with a working knowledge of the OHSAA's bylaws, the danger of bringing in these new players was immediately apparent. The organization's regulations simply do not allow for reclassification. A student only has four years of high school eligibility, regardless of whether they had even participated in sports during those four years. It would be impossible for COF Academy to be able to gain membership into the association if they used these players. OHSAA Bylaw 4-3-3 reads, "After a student completes the eighth grade or is otherwise eligible for high school athletics participation, the student may be eligible for a period not to exceed eight semesters taken in order of attendance, regardless of whether the student participated or is even eligible to participate in accordance with these eligibility bylaws." Another restriction is an age limitation, a straightforward bylaw that specifies, "Once a student attains the age of 20, the student will no longer be eligible for interscholastic athletic competition notwithstanding where that 20th birthday falls in relation to the sports season." Another bylaw adds further restrictions. "A student is considered a graduate when the student has completed the work required for graduation and is declared a graduate by the Board of Education or a similar governing board. Notwithstanding the fact the student may be age eligible and have [a] semester of eligibility remaining, a graduate is no longer eligible for interscholastic sports except for participation in the remaining contests of that semester [of graduation.]" But at the time, Johnson didn't know about those rules, and he didn't investigate any further.

"I don't know who he knew in New York, but next thing I know, we got kids from New York. I'm like, 'Well, who the hell are these guys? Who are these kids?'" Johnson had occasionally been involved in football matters in the past, but to Hall, this was Johnson's first major foray into affecting the on-field operations of COF Academy, and it wasn't the ideal scenario for Williams and Hall, who had been trying to build a certain type of roster and team. "Some of these kids were older than they should have been … I didn't know anything about these kids. I hadn't spoken to all their parents. I just look up and there are kids from New York that Roy's bringing in. I'm like, 'Roy, I don't know their parents. I don't know the situation. What are you doing?' It made me very uncomfortable."

To address these moments, Williams started a common refrain: "We gotta look out for the kids." During times when the coaching staff felt uncomfortable, they would often remind each other that they were in the business of improving the lives of the students involved, even when things felt strange. And around the same period, Johnson and the team received a communication from the Ohio Department of Education. Their paperwork had been processed and they were officially registered as a school, no visits or authentication required. "I remember seeing that email," he said. "Everything was in stone. We're good to go."

But not everything was good to go. COF Academy still needed a bigger squad. And between Hall and Johnson, they went looking for ways to expand it.

One afternoon in May, Tracie Baugus and her son, Keith "K.J." King Jr., were walking into a Columbus Walmart when Hall and Johnson approached them. "Hey man, you're a good-sized kid. We've got a bunch of professional guys working out if you want to get a workout in," Johnson told him. Later, he would say with confidence that his approach was perceived as friendly. They asked King if he played football, and he told them he played at Westerville North High School. The 6-foot-4, 238-pound defensive end looked like a player they wanted on the team, and they asked him if he had any college offers, explaining their new school and its impressive schedule. They promised they could land him a Division I scholarship, asked him what team he wanted to play for in college, and told him they could help him get there. Johnson thought they were portraying confidence. Baugus was alarmed.

"We didn't really know what to think at the time and had never heard of their school," she said. "We were freaked out about being approached in a parking lot." King gave them his cell phone number because, as his mom said, "What else do you do? He didn't know what to say. I didn't know what to say. You can ignore someone when they call you." The pair went into the Walmart, and when they walked back to their cars, they saw Johnson and Hall still sitting in an idling SUV in the parking lot. When they got home, Baugus googled them and COF Academy. She couldn't find anything. King never took them up on their offer, completing high school with Westerville North before playing football for Walsh University.

Between those types of interactions and their flashy schedule, it didn't take long for COF Academy to make a name for themselves among the football community in central Ohio (long before the press had any idea they existed). On high school football message boards, people began to take notice. And as they got more brazen with their outreach, other programs did too.

Tennyson Varney, the head coach of nearby Grove City High School at the time, said in 2018 that he had first heard of COF Academy earlier in the year when his players told him someone from the school had taken them on a trip to Easton Town Center to persuade them to leave Grove City. "They were recruiting my kids—calling them, picking them up, taking them on visits—and who knows what they were telling these kids," Varney said. "They convinced them they were going to get them to a Division I school. They told one kid they would get him re-classed as a junior so he could start his recruiting over again. It was bad. There's no other way to put it."

Bruce Ward, head coach of Gahanna Lincoln High School in 2018, said one of his players was contacted as late in the season as July 28, two days before fall practice began. "I think we're all on the same page with the fact that it ruins what Ohio high school football is," he said. "Most of us are not about trying to form the best team and recruiting kids. Ohio is too good at football in my opinion to have that type of mentality. Central Ohio is not the place for that."

Johnson didn't particularly care about the opinions of area coaches. To him, "everyone" recruits in one way or another. And for Williams, COF Academy was simply providing an alternative. He claimed their approaches were done "in a respectful way," and he believed the school was "offering a choice," just like any other private, religious school. "It's an opportunity," Williams said at the time. "If the family feels better to stay at their high school, no problem. Great. But some kids want a different challenge." He said he wished other coaches "would understand that we're not trying to steal their players."

Johnson, however, was more bullish about the recruiting project, and he never denied going after players on other teams. In fact, he felt it was the only way to field a competitive team. "We all know the OHSAA says it's illegal to recruit; we all know that," he said. "But we also know that recruiting is happening. You can watch and see."

He may not have cared about the opinion of fellow coaches, but Johnson was right: the OHSAA did indeed outlaw recruiting. The organization's bylaws detail rules for transfers and specify that students must change their enrollment and attend the new school in order to be eligible, though there were a variety of exceptions. Students who do not transfer according to the bylaws or meet an exception, however, were supposed to become ineligible during the second half of a season and OHSAA playoffs. Johnson simply claimed that everyone else was breaking those rules, so he would too.

Beau Rugg, OHSAA director of officiating and sport management at the time, found that claim frustrating. While he admitted it was a challenge to enforce recruiting rules, he made it clear that the school could not continue its brazen recruiting strategy if they wanted to join. "If they want to be a member, they've got to follow our rules and regulations," he said. "Recruiting is not following our rules and regulations. So they'll have to make the determination of how they want to progress with that … and what model they want to use. If they want to use a model of recruiting, that's not going to be one where they'll get through a probationary period."

Johnson knew what was against the rules, and continued to make claims that embellished the program's qualifications and lied about its methods. After a prospective membership meeting with the OHSAA, he promised administrators that

COF Academy did not recruit and would be able to meet all of the probationary standards of the OHSAA. Johnson boldly informed OHSAA staff that his school would win a state title the first year they were eligible to do so. Beyond issues with academics and recruiting, there are other rules required to complete a goal like that, such as offering at least two sports per season. Johnson had never planned any sport beyond football for the 2018 year, and soon dropped the idea of joining the OHSAA.

The recruiting incident was just one of many pitfalls that COF Academy would need to avoid before they could achieve any of their lofty goals, and it was one of many reasons why the organization kept a very close eye on the school through the end of the summer. To Johnson, that scrutiny was a slap in the face. Because in his eyes, he wasn't just building a football team or a school, he was creating the next great American institution. And in his mind, the issue of flaunting some regulations is a miniscule one. How can you create anything great without breaking a few rules?

"People are going to take this the wrong way, but I don't know how to put a school together without recruiting," he said at the time. "So of course we tell kids, 'Yeah, we're going to have a great football program.'... But we also offer the educational program we have to have. So I don't look at us any different than anyone else.... If you're good at ballet, you go to Juilliard. If you're good at art, you go to an art school. What I hope we bring to the table is saying, 'Yeah, I'm going to a sports-specific school where they do a lot of sports and do them well. But guess what? I'm also getting an education. And I'm going to college for free.' And that's okay. It's okay to master your craft, especially when the end goal is to get to college for free.

"I just don't understand what we were doing wrong."

4

NOBODY WILL PLAY THEM

At the very top of the list of priorities for COF Academy and the later years of Bishop Sycamore was the compilation of an impressive and eye-catching schedule. For the team, that goal made perfect sense. They claimed to be a vessel for attracting eyeballs to the players on the team, and there's no better way to draw attention than by playing a top-tier selection of opponents, even if they knew they would lose. But for those opponents, who knew they would be playing a school with no history, a list of unanswered questions, and an open admission that they would likely lose, what made the matchup attractive? Ultimately, the answer comes down to the system in which high school football teams operate.

For nationally ranked football programs, and even those approaching that stature, finding and scheduling willing opponents is a challenge. Expenses for traveling out of state add up quickly, and in-state opponents don't see value in playing a game that seems like a guaranteed loss. Some schools—mainly traditional powers and major programs—have formed leagues and conferences that help alleviate some of that difficulty. For instance, the Central Catholic League includes Columbus,

Ohio, schools Bishop Hartley, Bishop Watterson, St. Charles, and St. Francis DeSales. But those leagues are rarely large enough to fill an entire season's schedule, which means they have to look elsewhere. And when they do, schools like COF Academy can emerge.

For one fleeting moment, Bishop Sycamore even joined a league in an attempt to legitimize the illusion that they were a regular high school—or at least close to it. But even the league they chose to use for that illusion was an interesting one. Ahead of the 2020 season, Bishop Sycamore joined the TCAL, the Texas Christian Athletic League. With a messy league website that provides very little information and hasn't been updated since 2019, it's not easy to find any information on the league. The only evidence of the school joining the league came when they were briefly added to that website. Bishop Sycamore never even played any other member schools of the TCAL, all of whom are actually located in Texas. TCAL officials never returned any requests for comment, and the website quickly removed any references to Bishop Sycamore in the aftermath of the IMG game.

When a program is backed into a corner and has the option of scheduling an unknown entity or missing out on the exposure and revenue of a home game, the choice becomes easy for most athletic directors.

For traditional high schools in Ohio, this is even more so the case. Football is the only sport under the jurisdiction of the Ohio High School Athletic Association—the governing body of Ohio high school sports—in which not every program qualifies for the end-of-season playoffs. To determine which schools are included and which aren't, the association developed the Harbin System, a points-based formula named after its inventor, Jack Harbin. The system can be complex, but at its core is the common idea that teams are awarded more points for beating larger schools than they are for beating smaller schools. Each school is placed into one of seven divisions based on enrollment, from DI to DVII. No points are awarded for a loss. In order to avoid a disadvantage for teams that are unable to find 10 games in a season, the formula changes for teams that only play eight or nine, essentially averaging out their score as representative of a 10-game season. The system is relatively efficient at determining the value of wins, but it contributes to the scheduling issues that schools face. Top-tier teams in the best divisions struggle to find similarly sized schools to play, and attempt to avoid scheduling games that they think they will lose. But at the other end of the spectrum, playing a lower-level school also represents risk. Smaller schools are worth so many fewer points than their larger counterparts that scheduling one of these matchups can damage a team's ability to make the playoffs, even with a win. This tension often leads teams to consider seeking out-of-state opponents, whose enrollments are checked by the OHSAA to award points accordingly. But those out-of-state opponents bring us back to the first issue: a lack of funding.

The emergence of COF Academy in the spring of 2018 solved every problem for any athletic director the program reached out to. Roy Johnson knew all about these problems, and saw an opening for his team. He reached out to athletic directors with a simple proposal: as a small, up-and-coming program, they could offer an easy scheduling option, an easy opponent, *and* a boatload of points. That's because Johnson told those schools that COF Academy would be considered a DI or possibly a DII team. The number to qualify for one of those divisions changes each year, but in 2020 the smallest DI school had 604 boys; the smallest DII school had 378 boys. At no point in the history of COF Academy or Bishop Sycamore did either program have more than 30 or 40 students at any given time. The largest school in Division VII for 2020 had 121 boys. Not only would Johnson's programs never reach the size of one of the top divisions, they would be considered one of the smallest schools in the entire state. That meant, in reality, that if their status were to ever be determined by the OHSAA, games against Johnson's programs would be nearly worthless, accounting for the fewest possible points to the teams who played them. For the competition they were trying to play, that would be a dealbreaker. But there was another option.

They could embrace not being a school at all.

Rather than adhering to the OHSAA's regular processes, compiling the requisite information, and revealing their extremely small stature, Johnson and COF Academy simply declined to participate in the process. Eventually, there was no option for the OHSAA but to consider COF Academy to be a non-school. That ruling meant that matchups against them would count for nothing—on paper, they would be a bye week and on the field they would be playing glorified scrimmages. But, crucially, opponents wouldn't ruin their average Harbin score by playing them. In fact, the removed pressure from the game often gave those opponents a chance to rest players and let reserves play. COF Academy's status as a non-school was virtually no issue. There is no OHSAA rule that says teams must play schools. If a high school football program was able to schedule the Cleveland Browns, they would be well within their rights to play them. Amid this dynamic, most schools made the easy choice: they'd rather have a home game and the money that comes with it than listen to the concerns about a school that wasn't.

During the first COF Academy season, just one scheduled school—Lakewood's St. Edward—put in the effort to investigate what was happening with their would-be opponents.

Originally scheduled to host COF Academy, they were made aware that the team likely had closer to 40 students than the 750 they claimed. That difference proved to be enough to warrant canceling the matchup. They couldn't let their playoff aspirations be affected. But at an annual spring meeting held by the OHSAA after the 2018 football season, the athletic director of St. Edward chastised OHSAA employees for not making a determination on COF Academy sooner, stating if they knew that the game wouldn't have counted for points, they would have played them.

Johnson learned from the process. And when it came time to schedule games for Bishop Sycamore, he knew that portraying elements of education and enrollment was simply an unnecessary step. He stopped trying to claim he had 750 athletes, and didn't bother to make appropriate ODE filings or apply for OHSAA membership. He had learned that it didn't matter—notable schools would play him without any of that. The game was all that mattered.

Behind the scenes, there was no longer any pretense of being a functioning school or a traditional scholar-athlete environment, and paperwork was the last thing on anyone's mind. In games between OHSAA member schools, a game contract is required, but that rule doesn't apply when a game is played against a non-member school. Programs like Aurora and Massillon would issue game contracts to Bishop

Sycamore that were never signed, an issue that would have doomed most other matchups. The games were played anyway. Warren G. Harding High School required Bishop Sycamore to sign their standard contract, so it was signed in spite of Bishop Sycamore knowing they did not follow the regulations it required. The contract specified that "The constitution, bylaws, and regulations of the Ohio High School Athletic Association and the Handbook for Officials are a part of this contract..." and that, "The suspension of membership in the Ohio High School Athletic Association by either of the parties to this contract shall render this contract null and void." The contract was void far before it was signed by Bishop Sycamore administrator David Brown.

Whether it was related to COF Academy, Bishop Sycamore, his various business schemes, or his friends and family, one consistent throughline for Roy Johnson was the revolving door of people with whom he surrounded himself. Coaches and players came and went, sometimes in the same week. Business partners played an integral role for a brief moment and then disappeared. Only a handful of individuals were consistently involved with the programs year after year, and most stuck around for a single season. David Brown was one of those single-season characters.

The only evidence of Brown's presence comes during the 2020 Bishop Sycamore season, when he was sometimes listed as the athletic director and sometimes as the assistant athletic director. He emailed schools through the generic Bishop Sycamore email address, info@bishopsycamore.org, and was the one to sign the game contract with Warren G. Harding before their matchup. For other games, like those against Aurora and Massillon Washington, there is evidence that the schools sent Brown a contract, but that contract was never signed by Brown or anyone else. The games were played anyway.

Massillon was the first game of the 2020 season for Bishop Sycamore, after the cancellation of the St. Vincent–St. Mary matchup. One of the premier high school football programs in Ohio, Massillon Washington High School was home to Paul Brown, the founder of the NFL's Cleveland Browns and Cincinnati Bengals. The matchup against Massillon was a major boost for Bishop Sycamore, and a major boost for Brown. In fact, he was so excited he gave an interview to Chris Easterling of the *Massillon Independent* that ran in the newspaper the day of the game.

"Dave Brown has been associated with Columbus Bishop Sycamore's football program throughout its admittedly brief existence. The school's assistant athletics director is essentially the one who works hand in hand with the Centurions' head coach, Donald Anderson, and the rest of the staff," the story began. "That position gives Brown a unique opportunity to be a mentor. Not just for the roughly 40 players on Sycamore's football roster, but also its collection of coaches as well."

The interview took place over the phone. Easterling never met Brown in person. And according to Easterling's records, the phone number used for the interview was the same number that appeared on the game contracts for Bishop Sycamore. That number was also the cell phone number of Roy Johnson.

A year later, after the fallout from the IMG game, Easterling looked back on his article, puzzled. "If I remember correctly, Brown identified himself as an assistant athletic director at the school. I did the interview over the phone. I never physically saw him. Dave Brown was the name given to me by Nate Moore. That was the guy that Massillon went through to schedule the game," Easterling said. "In retrospect, this doesn't surprise me. During the week I was just praying [Bishop Sycamore] showed up. They were supposed to play St. V the week before and canceled it. There were some Massillon officials that had some trepidation. We don't really want to play them, but it's 2020. We have this weird schedule, no one will play us. They showed up, they provided a roster, they played the game, I thought, 'Okay, this is over and done with, I can move on with my life.' But I was hoping no one would find that story.... I had to write a story about the opponent leading into the game, it's over and done with, and now a year later it's a national story."

In retrospect, Easterling wished he had looked with more depth into the conversation. But for an overworked newspaper journalist on a deadline, an in-depth investigation of a seemingly innocuous interview is a lot to expect. "[Brown] was willing to talk. I was sort of hesitant to even write anything about them leading into the game," Easterling said. "Tim Stried [director of communications with the OHSAA] reached out to me and was like, 'Do you know about these guys?' It's not my best work."

What would possess Johnson to create Brown as a pseudonym? Perhaps he was trying to keep his name out of Bishop Sycamore wherever possible at the time, as his lawyers advised him to do when COF Academy collapsed. Maybe Johnson was concerned his name would be a detriment to scheduling schools, as athletic directors and coaches around Ohio may remember his name from COF Academy. His name does not appear on any emails related to scheduling or documents from the 2020 season—those documents always included either Andre Peterson or Dave Brown. Easterling has a theory. "2020, for them, they were playing the long game. They were like a Trojan horse. 'We'll play these legitimate programs, we'll show up and play Massillon, Ignatius, Aurora, we'll take our beating, and we'll use that to legitimize ourselves and in 2021 we'll pull our masks off.' If you read the quotes in my story from whoever I talked to, they weren't selling themselves in the same way they were selling themselves the following year to ESPN. They didn't brag like, 'We have seven Division I all-stars.'"

COF Academy and Bishop Sycamore opponents didn't just know they weren't playing a "normal" high school. Many were made aware that Johnson had recruited players that had already graduated high school and would not have been permitted to participate in OHSAA-sanctioned athletics, and they admitted it publicly. In a September 2020 interview with the *Massillon Independent*, athletic director and head football coach Nate Moore said, "They've got a bunch of post-graduates, probably the best way to say it." Two of the players who participated in the game against the Tigers that night, Elijah Montgomery and Antwaun Artis, had active felony warrants for their arrests at the time of the game. Due to an ever-changing and rarely accurate roster at both COF Academy and Bishop Sycamore, it's nearly impossible to tell how many overage players were involved at a given time, but at least Montgomery was 20 years old at the time of the matchup.

Athletic directors at the schools involved faced the exact same challenges with errant and missing rosters, but those athletic directors determined that they'd rather play than miss out on a home game, even if they would be putting their players on the field with 20-year-olds and players being sought by police. All football games come with inherent risk, but matchups with Johnson's team were a special case. In the case of Massillon, one player, Rager Els, ended up with a broken leg. The game wasn't held to any rules or regulations. It wasn't a matchup between two schools.

"I'm not going to defend Massillon here," Easterling said, "or any of the schools that played Bishop Sycamore in 2020. But I think they were left scrambling. Massillon had a Week 2 game and everything got changed on them. Nobody would play them, like nobody plays Ignatius, like nobody plays [St. Edward's]. It's the same scheduling issues they have year after year, and now it's exacerbated [due to the pandemic]. I sympathize with the schools. I've covered Massillon over the years, and no one will play them. So you're like, 'Well, we can't go without a game,' and it's take what you can get."

Moore declined to speak on the matter and superintendent Paul Salvino's office provided only a statement saying, "The District has put this behind us and am [*sic*] moving forward." Artis later pled guilty to robbery, a second degree felony. Montgomery was arrested in June of 2022, more than two full years after his warrant was first issued. He pled guilty to reduced charges of receiving stolen property and failing to comply with the order of a police officer.

Prior to Archbishop Hoban's 2021 game against Bishop Sycamore, Principal T.K. Griffith and athletic director and head coach Tim Tyrrell were made aware of at least one 20-year-old player on Bishop Sycamore's roster and informed that Johnson—acting as head coach at the time—had an active warrant for his arrest. They were also given evidence of players who had exhausted their scholastic eligibility, regardless of their age, in violation of what would be standard OHSAA rules. In response, Tyrrell said in a phone call, "You just saved my job." But the game happened anyway, and in an email after the fact, Griffith said, "We feel we must move forward with this contracted event. We appreciate your communication."

A year later, with Bishop Sycamore suddenly a highly scrutinized household name, Griffith had changed his tune. "Our people didn't realize—I didn't realize—to what extent that maybe they're not a school or not a legitimate entity.... I don't think any of us realized they're not what the ODE would call a legitimate high school." Griffith claimed he was not aware of any conversations about potentially canceling against Bishop Sycamore. "I feel like we weren't aware they weren't legitimate. I don't know if we even thought about it, we just knew it was the first football game of the year and Bishop Sycamore was coming up. I guess we had heard they had some good athletes or good players, but I don't think anyone thought about it to be honest with you. We've become so good at football that some people don't want to play us, so sometimes you have to reach out for games, which is pretty common when you start winning a lot … I don't remember anything startling or worrying about that game prior to it."

Griffith had been given evidence of 20-year-old players and a wanted head coach, but wasn't worried about it. Even with the benefit of hindsight, he stood by his decision. "I regret that they lied, I guess. I would say they lied. I don't think we were duped, because other people had them on their schedule. I feel bad for them if they were using kids and not providing them an academic environment to be held accountable to, I feel bad for all that, but I don't feel bad for us. We were just looking for a game … I don't think it gave us a black eye in any way."

The OHSAA had done what they could to make schools aware of who Bishop Sycamore was. But to the people running those schools, Johnson's teams were simply the next opponent up. They never even "thought about it." They were just "looking for a game."

Even the students lining up across from Bishop Sycamore paid more attention to the oddity of the program than administrators did. Hoban defensive tackle Bryce Sisak played in their season debut against Bishop Sycamore, and said they were abnormal from the beginning. "We didn't know much [about them]. We got a roster and we had film from 2019. We didn't have any film from the previous season. We normally, going into Week 1, have a bigger opponent. We'll have six to eight games of film from their last season. We only had like two games from the 2019 season. It was interesting." Sisak even said he knew Bishop Sycamore wasn't a school and assumed they were "like a prep school."

"We got a roster that was riddled with three- and four-star [recruits]. On paper, we should've gotten our asses handed to us. But then we came out in the game, our starting series, and they still had kids running out of the locker room. They had kids sharing helmets. It was all weird." Hoban won the game 38–0. A perennial football power in Ohio, Hoban was the reigning champion of Division II in 2021, having won four state titles in five years. Their players knew about highly recruited athletes, and they knew what those athletes looked like. They especially knew what it was like to play a good team. "We'd probably have, on average, one or two four-star recruits, and three to five three-star recruits," Sisak said. "It's normal for us to send anywhere between five to 10 kids to Division I [colleges]. But when I saw their roster, it didn't add up to me."

But not every school that Bishop Sycamore attempted to schedule fell for their fraudulent claims. For those who cared, a cursory look into the program showed everything that they needed to know. Willie McGee, athletic director of St. Vincent–St. Mary High School, canceled a scheduled game when he was informed of questions surrounding the team and could not verify athletes on the roster he was provided. Ryan Sayers, head coach of Northland High School in the Columbus City League, knew something was fishy from the moment he was approached.

"I met with them one time to talk about scrimmages and they were trying to promise me that they would pay me $5,000 just to scrimmage us. I said, 'No man, that's not going to work. No one pays $5,000 to someone just to scrimmage.' Then they said, 'You don't have a Week 1 game, we'll pay you $10,000 to play Week 1, and we'll get the game scheduled at Ohio State.' I said, 'There's no chance you're able to do that. You don't have $10,000.' He said, 'Trust me, we have the money.' These dudes were so sketchy. They couldn't explain school. They couldn't explain what classes were like. I don't know why anyone would believe them."

Hoban was "just looking for a game." Northland had higher standards.

5

TOO FOCUSED ON FOOTBALL

Behind the scenes, Roy Johnson struggled frantically to keep his project alive. But to the outside world, he and his team put on a strong face. COF Academy launched social media accounts that boasted about their schedule, and Johnson held a "media day" at SuperKick, an indoor training facility north of Columbus. The event was the program's introduction to the outside world, and an indication of what was to come. The day was frantic and unorganized. Johnson greeted the few media members who stopped by, and coverage was slim.

COF Academy's first and only head coach, Paul Williams, held a practice session while Johnson introduced himself to anyone he could find. Williams had found SuperKick as a solution to their lack of training facilities, and was plenty qualified to coach a football team. The former all-conference defensive back at Urbana University in Ohio spent 13 seasons as an assistant coach at Ohio Wesleyan University and worked for multiple arena football teams. But he also had the unique qualification of having coached in an environment much more foreign than the COF Academy landscape.

Between spells employed by Wesleyan, he spent four years in Kuwait helping to build the country's national football team. His LinkedIn page describes his role as "offensive coordinator, defensive coordinator, special teams coordinator, as well as the position coach for all positions. Recruited and evaluated talent. Taught all football skills and techniques." He would eventually become an advisor to the Kuwait Gridiron Football Federation. He helped develop a national flag football team that competed in two international tournaments, hosting the U-19 International Federation of American Football World Championship tournament in 2014, which included Canada, Mexico, Austria, Japan, Germany, France, and the U.S. Kuwait's beach-flag national team won the silver medal in the 2014 Asian Beach Games, the first American Football event recognized by the International Olympic Committee. So while Williams had never coached a high school team before, he was no stranger to a challenge.

Williams and Ulysses Hall had spent time together at Ohio Wesleyan, and Williams' place at the helm of the football program gave Hall the confidence to join the team. Hall said conversations among the coaches were the early anchors to the program, and that conversations were very different with and without Johnson in the room. Early in the process, it was clear that the team would struggle to be competitive. But the coaches tended to keep that to themselves. "I think sometimes Roy was a little bit unrealistic, but again, that's him trying to sell shit," Hall said. "But Paul and I had that understanding, man.... I'm like, okay, [Johnson] is a bit unrealistic with the timeline of how this is happening.... It's going to take some time to, you know, build a school."

But that realism didn't temper the spirits of Johnson—at least outwardly. Johnson clung to the schedule that made them catch eyes across the state, which included traditional Ohio powers Huber Heights Wayne, Cleveland St. Ignatius, and Lakewood St. Edward, as well as out-of-state programs such as North Allegheny and IMG Academy. "It's not that I want to necessarily keep it quiet," Johnson said at the time, wondering out loud if he waited too long to begin public relations and social media. "But we're going to stick out like a sore thumb because we took such a big schedule."

The first season included 12 games, two more than allowed by the Ohio High School Athletic Association. Immediately, Johnson admitted that gaining entry into the OHSAA could be an issue. And he knew from the beginning that the school's murky origins could lead to extra scrutiny. "Everything we do will be under the microscope," he said at that first open training session, which would be among their last at the facility.

The daunting schedule lent credibility to the program, but it also flagged unwanted attention from the OHSAA. By late summer, with games weeks away, OHSAA officials were publicly stating that they had not been in contact with Johnson or anyone else from COF Academy, warning that their games against championship-seeking Ohio schools may not count for postseason tournament qualification. To let the program join their ranks, the OHSAA needed to verify COF Academy enrollment numbers—a figure Johnson had put between 300 and 700, depending on who he spoke to and when. In reality, the team was made of about 30 kids at any given time, with no students present in the buildings they told the OHSAA served as classrooms.

Beau Rugg, director of officiating and sport management for the OHSAA, said at the time that he was "not real sure" why the school would be out of contact for months at a time if they were seeking membership. "They seem to communicate with individual schools all the time, and they won't communicate with us," he said. "I'll talk to one of our member schools on their schedule and they'll say, 'Oh, yeah, we just talked to them today,' while we're trying to get a hold of them to get information. I'm not sure what to make of that." In a common refrain, he said he had never seen a school attempt to build a football program at such a rate.

* * *

As Johnson and the Bishop Sycamore team flaunted rules, made up their own way on the fly, and generally bumbled through the creation of a football team, it's easy to forget that there are other, more ethical ways to create an athletics program in Ohio, particularly if the person starting that program takes the livelihoods of the children involved into consideration.

In 2017, Curt Caffey was hired as the athletic director of Patriot Preparatory Academy, a Columbus school with an enrollment of several hundred students. He had originally applied to be a basketball coach at the school, but was offered the AD role—the first of his career—and decided to take the job because his daughter had attended Patriot Prep. He saw it as a way of paying forward that experience. And less than two years into the job, he began undertaking his biggest challenge so far: launching the school's football program.

At first, the process seemed daunting. In the football-obsessed culture of Ohio and in the city of Columbus, where there's no shortage of competition and better-funded programs, his first task was to assemble a proposal for the school board. Caffey made sure to get that proposal exactly right, in order to set himself up for success. "It was a lot of research because there were a lot of projections. I wanted to at least get the board a ballpark [figure]." But cost wasn't the only factor that weighed on his mind. When building the program, one of his main worries was ensuring that whatever he created could sustain itself and wouldn't implode. He didn't want there to be any collateral damage. "I'm the type of guy and AD who likes to try to do it right. Because if you do it wrong and it collapses, a lot of people are going to be under that collapse."

With that in mind, Caffey's first big decision was to start at the middle school level and work the program up to a full high school team. It was simply unfeasible to responsibly start a team, ensure he had enough players, and establish all the baseline needs for a high school football team in less than a year. The process had begun just a few months after the 2018 season ended, which meant he was already working from behind many other schools, who have schedules and all of their logistics lined up a year in advance or more. With that in mind, he knew he had to organize three major elements before the program could exist: coaches, equipment, and a schedule.

To assemble his coaching staff, Caffey considered not just football qualification, but the personal backgrounds of the people he added to the football team. "I try to be a guy of good ethics and try to do it right, so when I was interviewing the coaches, in my mind I was thinking, 'What could go wrong with this individual?' In my conversations with them, I was also searching for righteousness—seeking individuals who also wanted to do it right, versus taking short cuts or having an outside motive beyond the kids." He ensured that his hires had their coaching certificates through the Ohio Department of Education, and had them learn CPR, how to operate a defibrillator machine, and some basic duties of an athletic trainer, because the small program didn't employ one. But most importantly, he ran a thorough background check. "To me, all the other stuff is Xs and Os, but I really wanted to find out the character [of coaches]. I didn't want to bring anyone on who had baggage or issues."

With a coaching staff established, he moved on to acquiring the team's gear, which was a bigger challenge than most might suspect. Even a few months after the football season, finding equipment—let alone affordable equipment—represented a major challenge. And along the way, if he had been less informed about that process, he could have found himself and his players in trouble. "You have to buy certified equipment, that's the big thing because there are people on the marketplace who try to sell you non-certified equipment. I heard a story recently where there was a vendor out in the marketplace selling non-certified helmets in bulk … and a kid was tackled in a game and hit helmets and one side of the helmet just crushed."

With unlimited funding, Caffey could have simply gone shopping. But in his estimates to the board, the highest end of that scale set the cost for equipping the team around $60,000. That was not money that the school had. Instead, he bought several helmets from secondhand sports stores and went through the process of getting them checked for certification. He found pads and uniforms discounted where he could, and used only a couple of footballs for the program's early days because cheaper bulk orders were backordered for months.

Finally, he could work on getting teams to play. With less than a year to set a schedule, he called in some favors with other athletic directors he knew. He settled for playing other teams "B or C teams" and begrudgingly scheduled games on Saturday mornings and other open time slots. Eventually, he finalized a seven-game schedule over the course of 45 days. "That was a big undertaking for the kids and coaches," he said.

To run the team, Caffey knew he had to charge a small fee. But unlike the hundreds or even thousands of dollars that other programs would charge, the Patriot Prep team would cost $150. Even that, to Caffey, was a fee worth taking very seriously. "About 95 percent of our kids are in what you would call the underprivileged category. So a lot of the families don't have the financial means to pay fees, so we have to find a way to offset them through other stuff. But interestingly enough that first year, which really says a lot, 98 percent of the parents did pay the fee with no problem.... We just have to maintain that level of fees and try not to go any higher."

Caffey also ensured that the program complied with OHSAA rules and regulations. He said before his arrival at the school, Patriot Prep had participated in an independent league that wasn't sanctioned by the OHSAA. Those days, he said, were disorganized and less responsible than he would have liked. Plus, without the OHSAA membership, players would miss out on opportunities. "The benefit there is tournament play—the kids get the opportunity to be part of a big tournament, to make all-league, all-district, player-of-the-year, and all those accolades. Being under the Ohio High School Athletic Association is big for the kids. And the other factor is really being under a governing body that scrutinizes and tries to do things right.... And then there's the validity [of joining]. OHSAA goes A through Z, in terms of checking the boxes."

With the team in place and a small roster filled out, Caffey's attention turned to ensuring that football didn't distract from the real purpose of Patriot Prep: education. "I'm a scholar-athlete kind of guy. I tell all the kids in my program, 'If you're not getting it done in the classroom or you're acting silly and disruptive in class, you really don't deserve to represent the school.'"

Caffey recommends to all of the school's coaches that every two weeks, players take around a grade sheet for all of their teachers to fill out. He says it lets the players stay on top of their grades and feel accountable for their progress while keeping teachers honest. Without the academic element of the program, Caffey doesn't find the sports side worthwhile. "We live in an era where so many young people in athletics think it's athlete-scholar, and I always correct them that it's scholar-athlete.... You can't just be all athletics and live in this world."

After the planned 2019 launch of the program was delayed due to the COVID-19 pandemic, Patriot Prep's first football team got off the ground in the 2022 season. They lost every game, which Caffey admitted was tough on everyone involved. But for him, there were more important things. The kids learned lessons from their experience, the football team made its debut, and the foundation was laid for the future. The players from that first team will continue to age through the program, serving as its first high school team within three years. "We've got a year under our belt. We saw a lot of things we could do better, but at the same time, we made it through. They didn't win, and I told the kids, 'The victory isn't always on the scoreboard. [It's about] the progression and what you learn.' We just tried to keep it positive."

* * *

Back in their apartments—or the floor of someone else's apartment, or a hotel room, or elsewhere—the COF Academy players were not seeing delivery on what had been promised to them. Like most students, Saadiq Mickens had heard the comparisons from Johnson. "It was supposed to be IMG, basically, of the Midwest," he told *The Athletic*. Mickens was one of many players to paint a picture of their living situation. After bouncing from hotel to hotel, most players settled in apartments furnished almost entirely by an air mattress. Some had televisions. Mickens wasn't miserable, but quickly got sick of eating the same salads on a daily basis, occasionally supplemented by home-cooked meals from wives of coaches and friends of the program. For Mickens, his COF Academy adventure took place moments from his previous high school, central Ohio's Westerville North, where he hadn't played football. But other players attracted to the program were taking larger gambles from further flung locations.

A handful of players on the team were recruited from New York, including the Bronx trio of Isiah Miller, Mario Agyen, and Rodney Atkins, on the same typical promise of college stardom.

Miller was first convinced to move to Ohio for COF Academy in a FaceTime call with friends on the team who bragged about their helmets and Adidas gear. He wanted a chance to play football in college and the idea of being able to play against IMG Academy was undeniably exciting, so he gathered his few belongings and bought a $56 bus ticket to a state he'd never visited.

Agyen, a friend of Miller's and fellow postgraduate player, was out of options in his attempts to keep playing football. The son of a Ghanaian immigrant, he was recruited through Twitter and promised that improving his GPA with the school could help advance his career. He and a friend drove to Pennsylvania to meet Johnson, and continued on to Columbus from there. A few hours later, he was on a practice field.

Atkins was one of the first New York players to arrive, and told the *New York Times* he helped convince several others to join him in Columbus. When Atkins' mother, Marysol, visited in the summer of 2018, she was shocked at what she found. "I walked into chaos," she told the *Times*, recalling two floors of players at a Baymont Inn being supervised by one staff member. She would stay three months, serving as a "team mom." But she wasn't the only mother to take notice of what was happening in Columbus.

Junior defensive back Damonte Ware had flown across the country for what he believed was a chance at playing in a high-profile football program. He paid $400 for a flight that took him from Belmont, California, to Ohio, where he was expecting to get a reimbursement from Johnson. But after just a few weeks, his mother, Miesha Ware, hadn't heard anything from Johnson about that money—or anything else. Furious about the lack of communication, she began investigating for herself, learning that Damonte and other students weren't taking classes in a classroom, as had been promised. She bought him another $400 ticket (also not reimbursed) and brought him home in mid-September, making him one of the few players to leave the program. "They neglected his education, and they've been having them stay in these hotel rooms," she said. "[Johnson] promised him this and promised him that and didn't do any of it."

There is no singular, representative story of the players' lives during that first year. Some players hated their time in Columbus, complaining of a lack of structure, boring and repetitive meals, and an inconsistent housing situation. Players said they were kicked out of at least two hotels, with brief stints staying in cabins outside of the city in an area with no cell phone reception and at a friend of the program's house, where dozens of players shared one shower.

Like their fleeting commitment to SuperKick, they would be introduced to a new location that was promised to be a regular school facility, only to never return. They would hold one-off practices at parks or drop by a neighborhood library that served as a classroom for the day. Occasionally, they would take tours of vacant lots where Johnson promised that there would one day be a school building. Once, they visited a fancy workout facility that was said to be their new home and were given key cards before leaving and never going back. Players told stories of other students and even coaches getting into fights in the tense environment. Years later, some players would say they stole food or saw others do so. Some players pushed back at that idea, claiming those players were simply bored of the daily hot dogs or salads. Eventually, they settled down at an apartment complex with televisions and air mattresses to themselves.

Although he acknowledged that the food situation wasn't what he had hoped it would be, Johnson has no sympathy for the kids who complained. He believes they should be thankful for what they had. In his mind, those who expressed their unhappiness in interviews—he believes they're lying—were simply looking to be in the headlines. "Mrs. Peterson had cancer. She would literally go to chemotherapy, leave chemo, come to where we were and cook dinner for these guys every night. That's how you thank her and repay her? By getting your five minutes of fame and saying you only got one hot dog in five days. It's just so disrespectful to the people who gave you opportunities." Do those things make it okay for him to have overpromised and under-delivered? "I don't know, because it was good food," he said, breaking into uproarious laughter. "They ate better than I did."

One day, Johnson went out to his car and claimed he found a homeless man stealing his belongings. When he "started getting into a fight" with the man, players ran out from inside and joined in, beating the man. The man allegedly had Johnson's phone, wallet, jewelry, and other items, and prompted more aggressive action from the group when he began waving around a hatchet. "One of the players punched him in the face," Johnson said. "These kids are all from bad neighborhoods, so when one fights, we all fight. So he got beat up. After he got beat up for a little bit, I said, 'Hey guys, let him up.' I told him, 'Give me my shit back, or it's going to be a long day.' He took off running and we chased him down again and one of the players tackled him and we surrounded him.... I told the kids, 'You know why he's acting like that? Because his daddy didn't whoop his ass.' So I started whooping him with my belt until he gave me my stuff." Johnson claims the man called police, who arrived and didn't take a report after the man told them Johnson "beat me like a slave," which Johnson found hilarious. "I had to laugh. I was like, 'Now that's funny.' But in all actuality, I did whoop him with my belt like a slave, so what he said was very true." There was no police report detailing the incident.

To Johnson and Greg Sullivan-Crockett, the incident was hilarious, not traumatic. Sulllivan-Crockett was one of Johnson's favorite students, a quiet lineman Johnson called in the middle of retelling that story. He asked the former player to name his favorite COF Academy memories, and Sullivan-Crockett said, "Beating up that geek." It was, however, a tough incident to explain later. "The fact he got his ass whooped, I don't really feel bad for," Johnson said. "The thing I do feel bad about is that it's another thing that, due to unfortunate circumstances, I subjected these kids to. And now I have to call every parent and explain what happened."

But there were funny moments that didn't involve physical violence, too. One Friday night, hours after a game, Johnson woke up in the Ohio Wesleyan University lodging where the team was staying. He yawned and did a room check well after midnight, and found many of his players missing. "Roy figured out that they had snuck out, so we're driving around campus looking for them," Sullivan-Crockett said. "First, we see some of our players walking down the street with some girls. This man [Roy] pulls up on the curb," he said, amid interjected swerving sound effects, "and terrifies the shit out of them. 'Get the fuck home right now!' They froze like deer in the headlights and walked home all quiet like."

The evening didn't stop there. Some of the players told Johnson that their teammates were partying at a nearby campus bar. Johnson grabbed Sullivan-Crockett (who had stayed home) and went searching. He and his offensive lineman arrived at the bar, where the pair claim Johnson swiftly dispatched a pair of bouncers before storming the stage. "The bouncers were like, 'Man, you can't just come in here.' I was like, 'Bro, does it look like me or the people behind me are playing?' So I walked in, walked up to the DJ booth, shut the music off, and said, 'If anybody in here is from COF, you better get the fuck out of here.' I turned to the owner and was like, 'You got minors in here drinking.' Matter of fact, I grabbed the mic and said, 'This whole party is shut down.' I shut the entire bar down. I pulled the wires out of the speakers. Managers and stuff came up to me and were like, 'You can't shut my bar down.' I was like, 'You have minors in this motherfucker.'" He claims he made enough of a scene that the bar shut down and police were called. But he found his players.

"We get back to the hotel and they were like 'My bad, Coach, I'm sorry,'" Sullivan-Crockett said. "He was like, 'I don't want to hear all that, get ready to run.'" Johnson made the players run until 4:00 AM. The team laughed about it afterward.

On the field, there was less laughing. The team was not only pieced together with players who had never met each other—sometimes until days or hours before a game—it was much smaller than the coaches would have preferred. "The first season, in the week leading up to the game, we're like, 'Man, we're only gonna be able to fill [out a] team of about 20, 30 guys,'" Hall said. "And they're not the best players … a lot of guys playing both ways. But it was no problem. There are some schools that run a football program and they only got 22. All you need is 11 on offense, 11 on defense. So we were gonna make it work." It was a far cry from the 500 or even 300 promised by Johnson at various times. And he was frustrated. "Roy wanted more," Hall said. "I'm like, 'Well, Roy, I don't know what else to do at this point.' We have who we have; let's go."

The team started a daunting 12-game schedule on August 17, 2018, at Fortress Obetz. Their opening game against visiting Canadian school Clarkson North ended in a 35–0 defeat, one of COF Academy's three scoreless games on the season. Ohio newspaper *The Richland Source* described Clarkson's "impenetrable defensive effort" in the rout. The next five games were largely the same outcome, resulting in defeats of 45–20, 42–6, a competitive 26–14, 35–0, and 35–14.

As the season progressed, the coaching staff dwindled. Johnson's lack of funding meant that many, including Hall, weren't being paid. Sometimes, Johnson tracked down enough cash to give certain coaches a payment or two. That rarely included Hall. Former Ohio State receiver Jeff Greene served briefly coaching receivers and defensive backs. When he was lured to the program by Johnson and Williams, he said it "seemed like a great idea," but said he never learned anything about a contract and was never paid. "They just kept saying they'd get back to me." By mid-September, after coaching for free for a few weeks, he quit the program, saying at the time that "no one knows what's going on" and that he and others owed money by Johnson couldn't reach him.

But pressure on the program wasn't just coming from within. One night, Johnson claims he came home to find spray-painted messages on his garage door. Other days, people would bang on his door and run away. He said he called the police, but never filed a report. At the time, he worried about his family. "And it hurts when you have a one-and-a-half-year-old at home that doesn't understand," he said. "And now his mom is upset." Players received similar harassment, including threatening messages. Johnson advised them to stay quiet and avoid incentivizing "copycat behavior."

"I told the guys, 'Just keep it quiet.' We used it as motivation," he said. "Most of these guys are from really rough neighborhoods. So I told them, 'You guys shouldn't be intimidated by text messages. Where y'all are from, people tell you to your face. So don't worry about a text message.' Meanwhile, I'm going inside and praying on my hands and knees that nothing happens." Fortunately, none of the problems advanced beyond threats and vandalism.

Finally, in Week 7, the team got their only win of the season in a 14–13 victory over Michigan's Brother Rice, a team that went 7–4 on the season. After that win, they lost four more in a row before the season finale, a trip to St. Frances Academy in Baltimore. But that game was over before it began. The team traveled all the way to the east coast, but players were frustrated. After enduring their living conditions and a brutal season of defeats, they didn't want to play anymore. Many members of the coaching staff, after continuously not being paid, had quit. They never fielded a team for the game, an emblematic ending to the lone season of COF Academy football.

Although the players felt short-changed by the program, Johnson somehow felt the same way about the players. When he read the New York trio's interviews in 2021, he said he reached out to ask, "Is there anything I can do now?" But in the moment, he felt anger and frustration that they, in his view, didn't ask for help earlier. He didn't reach out to them either, but feels, for some reason, that it was their responsibility to do so. "You mean to tell me that all those guys in the *New York Times* article, all the guys from New York who got here, that was four years ago and in four years you never reached out? There was never a 'Hey, can you help me?' Nothing? All this stuff is going on, and you're not really saying anything."

For the coaches, the experience was as much a letdown as it was for the players. Hall said he and Williams are "still putting our lives back together." He felt sympathy for the many people who had been promised a "cut" of the COF Academy earnings that would come someday. They never arrived. After his time at COF Academy, Williams became the safeties coach for Alderson Broaddus University. He now works in security management for UPS. Hall continued to find a variety of football coaching jobs, and is currently the defensive line coach and recruiting coordinator for John Carroll University.

In retrospect, players had varying feelings about their experience in that year. Bryan Davis, a tall and athletic receiver from North Carolina, came to Columbus with a dream of playing in the NFL and the hope of improving his grades. He called his experience "mixed," but said that he was able to keep up on his grades in Ohio, taking classes regularly and focusing on football and school rather than outside distractions. It was a lesson he valued, and he believed the experience was worth his time. He said his teammates and coaches "taught me real life," and he treasured memories of grilling and rapping with his friends, even with everything swirling around them. "It was a lot of good things [but] a lot of hard times," he said. "I didn't really focus on that. I was too focused on football."

Of all the players who have a right to look back on their COF Academy days in anger, Rodney Atkins tops the list. Rather than launching an NFL or even college football career, his time in Columbus was one of many steps that led him to the psychiatric ward at Jacobi Medical Center, where he spoke to the *New York Times* in 2021. After returning to the

Bronx in 2019, he fixed up a house belonging to his grandmother before she died, renting rooms to make money. His football career didn't pan out, but he doesn't blame Johnson or COF Academy. "It's an experience," he said. "You can always take pros and cons out of everything. I still think it's a good opportunity, a good vision. But you need money to make the dream work, and there was a lack of."

It was only a matter of time before that lack of money caught up to Johnson. And while the on-field performance of the team crumbled, so too did the infrastructure in which it had existed for its brief life. And within weeks of the season ending, Johnson was battling legal issues on all fronts, speaking with the Secret Service, and disappearing once again.

6

WHERE SPORTS BECOMES EVERYTHING

As the teenage son of a single mom growing up on Chicago's South Side in the late '90s and early '00s, Tyrre Burks found the first refuge of his life in sports. And in that environment, that was a fortunate discovery. "Where I grew up, you either played sports or you were in the streets. I found sports."

It didn't take long for sports to consume Burks' life. He wrestled, played football, ran track, and swam throughout the year, attending Carver Military Academy, a public military high school situated in what he described as "one of the two remaining projects in Chicago." But it was football that truly gave Burks the key to a new life, a "safe space" where he found his first glimpses of male leadership and the pursuit of excellence.

"I grew up in a place where safety was a luxury. So finding a safe environment where you could grow and develop was … really important," he said. "By freshman year of high school, I had never thought about what I wanted to be. I couldn't even think that far ahead. So when I get invited to wrestle and I'm in practice, for the first time I have a male giving me encouragement. I'm being seen for the first time.

Someone wants me to do something positive and they want me because they feel like I have the potential for something. That feels really good, to actually have someone recognize you for something you haven't done yet. They see something in you."

Burks remembers the first time he pinned someone in a wrestling match. The reaction of his coach and teammates opened his eyes and his world view. It was the first time he'd ever won anything, and it changed his life.

"That's where sports becomes everything. All around you, there is nothing else. There is no other positivity happening. When you go home, mom is working three jobs and tired and running around. She loves you and provides for you, but she doesn't know what you're going to be either, because she doesn't know what's going to happen to you when you leave the house. All she can do is the best she can with what she can provide you and hope that you surprise her with wanting to do more. You realize, 'This is it. This is the only place in my life where I'm getting this, where I have an opportunity.' Everyone in the NFL that looks like me came from these parts. Most of these guys came from the hood, and they came from fatherless homes. That and rapping are the only examples I can see that people like me are having success."

The combination of his early success and his drive to achieve came with a newfound hope that someone would discover him. Maybe someday, he thought, the right pair of eyes could pull him out of the South Side world he'd always known. "You always just have that hope. Your coach is saying, 'This opportunity is going to get you this chance,' and when you have very little hope, the chance is all you need. It's all you have. So you're going to cling to that chance and do everything you can to make it happen. You're extremely vulnerable."

Dr. James Patrick Lynch is the executive director of athletics at The School District of Philadelphia and has been a vocal proponent of youth athletic reform across the country. For Lynch, many of the problems in youth sports—from elementary school to the college level—come from the uniquely American obsession with winning. Rather than creating a health-focused environment where kids can learn skills, improve their physical abilities, and establish a healthy baseline of exercise and competition, the scoreboard becomes the focus far too early.

"Our country is still very much focused on winning, even at the youth levels, which creates that mentality as they grow. And it's why you see schools like Bishop Sycamore spring up. It's going to take a lot of work to reverse course. We have certain things in place but we don't have all the players at the table. We still have college coaches who, out of one side of their mouth, say, 'We want our kids to play 10 different sports and sample,' and out of the other side of their mouths they're telling kids they [won't be] doing anything except playing football."

Lynch also warns of what he calls "street agents"—people crawling throughout the system who have enough knowledge to be dangerous but not enough ability or connection to be beneficial. Those characters are often family friends, neighbors, uncles, or anyone else loosely connected to kids and programs. These street agents tell kids they don't have to worry about school because they're good enough to get a scholarship and play in the NBA or NFL. And without someone to correct them, they present an extremely appealing plan for a teenager. "Next thing you know, the kid can't make his grades, can't get a scholarship, and doesn't go to college," Lynch said. "That just becomes even more detrimental to the society cycle."

Burks is no stranger to stories of kids getting trapped in that cycle. He recalls a friend who coaches an inner city Chicago team that actively tries to send kids to college on legitimate scholarships. But even in that scenario, they find it extremely challenging to make opportunities stick.

"In 2019, he sent something like 16 kids to Division I and II scholarships on full rides. It was a huge accomplishment. The very next year, all but one of those kids was back home. When those kids get there and they fail, they have no confidence and they don't believe in themselves or feel that they're worthy. They got pushed through the [Child Protective Services] system, they never got held accountable for anything, they're still reading at a third-grade level, and they can't hack it at, say, Georgia Tech. We're talking about real schools. They're going to Georgia Tech, Virginia Tech, UCLA—really good schools."

In his childhood, education "didn't mean much" to Burks and his classmates. Now, as he provides a "world-class education" for his son, he sees the massive advantages that come with being properly educated and prepared for adulthood. It's a luxury that many students across the country—particularly minority students in disadvantaged backgrounds—can't even dream of, and it's why he grows angry when he hears of schools like Bishop Sycamore dismissing education as a tertiary goal.

"That pisses me off, especially because I know that most of these kids are African American kids. As a coach, if my main objective is to make sure that these kids become successful in whatever they do, I want to do everything I can to make sure that they're in an environment that's going to allow them to not just get to the next level, but thrive at the next level."

For Tom Farrey, the founder and executive director of the Aspen Institute's Sports & Society Program, the Bishop Sycamore story represents "a big, shining example of how school sports in this country have lost their way." Farrey's program aims to bring together leaders for conversations to help sports serve the public interest. Throughout his years working in youth sports reform, that element of competition over all else has been a recurring theme. And at Bishop Sycamore, he saw "a scenario that was dominated by entertainment interests and not educational interests."

Farrey said, "There's a reason they're called school-based sports—school is supposed to come first. But when you're aggregating your talent from all over the place for the purposes of downstream financial return on investment for different actors—from coaches to players to schools themselves—it's no longer educational activity, it's professional sports activity poorly constructed."

With the encouragement of his mother and a knack for football, Burks was one of the lucky few to turn his talents into a career. He earned a scholarship to play football at Winona State University in Minnesota, where he was an all-conference wide receiver in his junior and senior seasons. Perhaps more importantly, he earned his degree. He parlayed his college success into a brief professional career, playing one season in Europe and three more in the Canadian Football League before injuries forced him out of professional play.

But Burks knows his story isn't the typical tale of a young boy in a bad situation finding a dream in sports. And now, as he runs Players Health (an organization he founded to mentor students and help athletic programs mitigate risk) and helps his own son grow through the ranks of youth sports, he sees more clearly than ever the opportunity for exploitation that comes with the desperate situations of kids like he once was.

"You have to start with the environment kids are in—areas like New Orleans, Baltimore, Chicago, Detroit—there are certain parts of those cities where there's very little hope. My son goes to school here in Lakeville, Minnesota, and all of these kids only talk about what college they're going to. It's progressive conversation and hopes and dreams and it's constantly thought about. But when you grow up in an environment where—daily—people are being shot and killed and there's drugs and fear, you only live for that day and that moment."

For kids who grow up with the combination of a low-income household, an underprivileged area, a lack of male role models, and an uncertain path into the future, a coach can become elevated to a new level. And at that level, Burks said, it's easy to take advantage of the children who are relying upon you.

"Those coaches are more than just coaches, they're father figures. That's the first positive influence that these kids have ever had in their whole lives. So the amount of power, influence, and say that a lot of these coaches have in those neighborhoods is massive. This is the first time you've ever had any kind of success in your life, period."

For many athletes, that relationship with a coach or other mentor can be life-changing. But for some it can be devastating, exploitative, or even abusive. "I know that, within communities where I grew up, incidents haven't been reported because of how our communities are set up," Burks said. "I know, anecdotally, that it makes sense for a lot of physical, emotional, and sexual abuse to happen in settings like this, where the athlete perceives that this one individual has the key to their future."

Curt Caffey of Patriot Prep has been working with young athletes for decades, including his own daughter. He helped build the school's fledgling football program and said he sees plenty of people taking advantage of young athletes, especially in underprivileged communities like the one his school belongs to. For him, the first step is to ensure that students are surrounded by coaches with a higher quality of character. "One of the areas of great impact is the behavioral factor of the adult coaches," he said. "You have to really try to screen coaches in a way that there's not a lot of underlying or hidden agendas as it relates to taking advantage of the kids. When I think of how some of these associations or programs are pulling kids in—especially in AAU basketball—it's just terrible. I think there needs to be another level of education to the parent, in terms of the reality of their son or daughter making it to X level. I'm sure there are statistics out there that show what a very small percentage make it there."

Caffey said he's also seen a lot of "very persuasive" coaches who play on the emotions of the parent rather than the student, a strategy that can sometimes be more effective, especially when trying to make money. "We charge $150 and some parents cry about that, but yet they have their kid playing AAU and they're paying $700 to travel and they have to pay for housing, etc. So I think the emotional factor is where some of these coaches home in on those parents and they see, 'Mr. Caffey is really supportive of his daughter. I think that's one we can tag and get that $700.' And then they promise the dreams to these individuals."

Burks advises parents and students to make a deep assessment of a school, program, or coach before entrusting them with the safety of a child. He said questions such as, "Where are they traveling? How organized are they? What are the communication mechanisms?" are all elements that should be easily identifiable and coordinated with parents. In situations that lend themselves to negative outcomes, those organizational aspects don't exist.

But the very first recommendation of a major red flag for Burks is an easy one: "If one person is running the whole show, that's an issue."

At the programs he launched, Roy Johnson was very aware of his students' backgrounds and their lack of options. But after the fall of Bishop Sycamore and witnessing children's lives being affected by choices he made after promising them the world, Johnson had a different perspective than Burks. With two children of his own—which he called "cool" and "different"—Johnson looks back on many of the kids he recruited and sees not exploitation, but a reason to blame parents.

"You have a different type of respect for people when you're dealing with their children. But at the same time, you also have a certain amount of—I don't know how else to say it, so I'm just going to say it—disgust. My son will never get to the point where he's a senior in high school and has a 1.5 GPA. It's amazing how parents have nothing to say until a camera shows up and all the sudden they're parents of the year," he laughed.

It annoys Johnson that students weren't more appreciative of what he gave them. For kids who weren't appreciative enough, it was just another sign for Johnson of parenting failures.

"It's just so disrespectful to the people who gave you opportunities. But I can't expect any better from you because, guess what? You were raised in a house where your mom let you get a 1.5 GPA." What if Johnson's son found himself in such a position one day? "That would be terrible. My son would never be in that position. Not at all."

If kids had such a bad time at Bishop Sycamore, Johnson asserted, they didn't have to be there. Doesn't that just confirm that a lack of options can lead children seeking a better life to make decisions that aren't in their best interests? Doesn't he agree that his players were only there because there wasn't a better alternative for them?

He said, "I know there wasn't, 'cause if there was a better alternativc, you know what? They could leave. They were here for free."

7

A NON-SCHOOL PROGRAM

In the spring of 2018, the grand plans for COF Academy's lavish academic and athletic campus were actually moving forward. Although his services could have been used almost anywhere, renowned developer Mike Egan had helped assemble a team that could make Roy Johnson's plans a reality, and he did so because of the presumed purpose of the school. "I convinced a lot of contractors and people to get involved, and they all really wanted to get involved and really put their time and effort in," he said in early 2019. "And a lot of it wasn't even charged. A lot of it was, 'We get the cause. We want to be supportive and help.' It was never about the money."

Jeff Kellam felt the same way. Kellam, the owner of Indiana-based construction company Kellam Inc., was also drawn to the project because of the benefits of helping a community. And although the plans were lofty, the AME Church's involvement lent an air of credibility to the plans. Kellam said he remembered one meeting in which Rev. Taylor Thompson stood up and declared Third District resources could back a debt of several million dollars. Everyone involved was ready for Phase 1, which would be the only phase of the project to ever be touched.

The job began with clearing the trees on the property donated by New Salem. At the time, the goal was to clear enough space that work could begin on the football field, which they still aimed to have done by August or September so that COF Academy could play home games on the site of its future campus. It was a relatively large amount of work, but the type of work Kellam had done many times. His company was there to clear the trees so that more heavy development work could begin. And still, all involved felt certain that there was someone other than Johnson behind the entire project. "Everyone at the AME Church and New Salem church ... there was no doubt that everyone knew we were out there working on that site on their behalf—everyone," Kellam said. "Everybody knew that we were out there doing that work."

At that point, as mentioned earlier, the federally protected Indiana bat was discovered nesting in trees scheduled for removal, and the project came to a stop. With no other option, work was over before it began in earnest. "I hate those things. I just want to get a BB gun," Johnson said in a 2019 interview, laughing out of frustration, mimicking the action of shooting bats with a gun.

Until the bats paused construction, the parties involved felt good about how things were advancing. But in mid-2018, communication between Johnson and the church dwindled.

Emails became cryptic, and Johnson stopped hearing news about financing from the banks he and the church had been in talks with. He was, however, still receiving regular communications, including detailed financial documents, from Rev. Thompson. "The spring flew by," Johnson said. "Suddenly, it's June, July, and we're not getting calls back. It's kind of hard to pinpoint when I thought, 'Oh no.' But I never really thought, 'Oh no,' because people are still flying out and working. So it was kind of like, 'Well, we're fine.'"

That summer, as Johnson built his team, the church quietly distanced themselves from the project. In July, the AME Church Third District added a statement to their website that claimed the church "has not authorized any person, whether they be officers, staff, pastors, or anyone associated with the Third District to commit the Third District, in any form or fashion, to any activities of the COF Academy." By the time anyone noticed the post in September, Johnson had known for weeks that the church's involvement in COF Academy was over—or at least he had inferred. He hadn't heard from anyone in weeks. He had a hard time breaking the news to people like Egan, who had dumped a lot into the project. "I spent countless hours in travel and convincing others to get involved because of the cause," Egan said. "I had personal conversations with the administrators within the AME Church about this project. And then to find out that people, including the bishop, had said that they have denied it is just very complex for me. I don't understand it at all. It's very disappointing."

Johnson claimed to be completely blindsided by the statement. He said he tried to give the church the benefit of the doubt for months, staying quiet instead of raising a stir because he couldn't believe the sudden change in direction. He even said he met with Young in person to discuss the situation. "When you hear that, you think 'Oh, that must be something else. That must be a mistake.' You go from there to still having conversations and people still coming in and knocking down trees and still moving forward. We had a meeting in Cincinnati with the Bishop and said, 'You can't say that.' They said whatever reason they gave and they took it down. So after they take it down, we're okay, correct? They took it down." The website did indeed remove the post in the fall of 2018, but it wouldn't change their attitude toward the situation. They continued to ghost Johnson and the program.

For a period of time, even Jay Richardson, 50 percent of the Richard Allen Group and Johnson's longtime friend and business partner, denied affiliation with the program. Although his signature was nowhere to be found and he was never physically present at COF Academy events, Richardson was listed as the school's superintendent in official Ohio Department of Education filings and Johnson confirmed his involvement in the establishment of the program. But when contacted about the story, Richardson took the route of combative denial. In angry Twitter messages, he would claim "no legal connection" to the program.

Meanwhile, well aware of the church's stance, Johnson wasn't deterred from the project, and it didn't change his behavior. He didn't tell the coaches and players that the church had disappeared. He didn't announce that the school would be shutting down. And he continued using the church's name for added credibility. To back up his ability to pay the rental agreement for the team's home field, Johnson emailed Jared Adkins, Fortress Obetz operations manager at the time, financial statements from the AME Church. The email came on Thursday, August 23, well after the church had denied any affiliation with the program. "Here are the financials (5 months bank statements, YTD Financials) and I sent you a dropbox attachment with the fly through of the Easton school project. Thanks for everything!" Johnson wrote.

Looking back on those months, he's still not sure why he didn't react differently. If he could do it again in a different way, he said he would. "The day the church started acting stupid and all these people were pulling out … I'd have sent all them fools home in the middle of the season," he said, referring to his players. "When I knew that they were officially done with it, it was done, they didn't want anything to do with it, I would have sent everybody home. 'The season's over.' I would have canceled the season, closed everything up, called it a day."

So why didn't he? That's more challenging for him to answer. "How much of it was wanting to help everyone out and how much was pride? How much was like, 'Man, I know I can get this right,' or, 'If I can get this together I can say, look at what I did?' How much of it was ego? I don't know. That's such a tough question to answer. You've got to have some kind of pride and ego to even attempt to do something as crazy as this. You don't just do it because you want to help people. If I just want to help people, I can go down to a soup kitchen and hand out soup. So some of it has to be ego and pride, I wouldn't dare sit here and say, 'Zero.' But how much of it is actually wanting to help? There are people who suffered from this that had nothing to do with it—my kids. They're not getting as much as they should be getting because I'm out here trying to make sure these things happen."

In spite of his kids or his livelihood or the rules or pending litigation, Johnson persevered. And his next battle was with the organization he had attempted to join.

A routine duty of the OHSAA staff was to confirm enrollment counts for non-member schools that played member schools during the football season. Schools in question are typically from other states, which makes the process simple: contact that state's board of education, request the official enrollment count and move on. It was rare that OHSAA investigators ran into issues with the process. Occasionally, Canadian teams came with different rules and regulations pertaining to their schools. Sometimes, administrators took their time responding. But for those at the OHSAA who looked into COF Academy's status in 2018, Johnson presented a unique and unprecedented issue.

From the beginning, he could not confirm the total enrollment of the school; his number varied from 400 to 800, a massive difference for COF Academy's opponents. On the high end, a number like 800 would guarantee the team counted as a Division I school, providing the maximum amount of playoff points. Even a smaller enrollment number could put the school at Division II or III, which would be promising for top-tier programs that struggle to find games. But anything lower than that, and the points simply wouldn't be worthwhile to the big programs. Regardless of the final number, the OHSAA needed this information, and every day of delay caused consternation to the member schools on COF Academy's schedule.

Staff members vented about their frustration with Johnson and the conflicting information they were receiving, which immediately raised a red flag. It was hard to believe that a program could have several hundred students in its first year. The figure was simply too unrealistic, and the space required to provide an education to that many students seemed too great. For a school of hundreds, there had to be more information readily available. A building would be well under construction, or already built. There would be more buzz surrounding the program. COF Academy was in Columbus, the same city as the OHSAA headquarters. But no one in the building had ever heard about an influx of hundreds of students to a brand new school.

The situation led to an internal debate among OHSAA staff members. Did COF Academy really have that many students? What was the potential harm of giving them OHSAA sanctioning as a DI school if they were not? And if they didn't have that many students, how many did they actually have? Some staff members felt an investigation was outside standard OHSAA purview—no one remembered ever balking at a school's stated enrollment before; they had always accepted the number provided. But ultimately, no school had ever put the OHSAA in this position before. Without precedent, it was determined that more work would have to be done, and they would not take COF Academy at their word. In response, Johnson told the OHSAA he could provide applications for at least 500 students to prove their enrollment, but applications alone do not prove a student is in a school. OHSAA investigators decided the easiest way to verify the presence of 500 students at a school would be to visit the school itself. It would be readily apparent if that many students were around, and would at least help efforts to ballpark a realistic number. The thought that COF Academy might not be a school at all had not yet crossed the minds of the OHSAA staff. Games were underway, so clearly there were some number of students at the school.

But in an unannounced visit to 112 Jefferson Avenue, the listed address of COF Academy, all that could be found was an AME Church building. Johnson had frequently mentioned the church in conversations with the OHSAA, and claimed it was the reason they were able to draw so many students. But inside the building, it was clear there was no school in session, especially not for 500 kids. People inside confirmed there was no school there, and no one knew anything about COF Academy. Days later, the decision to declare COF Academy a non-school program followed. On September 21, the OHSAA officially announced that they did not consider COF Academy to be an academic institution. It was the first domino to fall in the swift downfall of the program.

On September 26, 2018, the Ohio Department of Education followed the OHSAA's lead by opening an investigation into COF Academy. They reached the same conclusion, which resulted in the program losing their charter on October 18. In a letter sent to the program, the ODE said, "[Documents] identified Christians of Faith Academy would begin operation on August 14, 2018, and students would be in session on September 26, 2018, the date the visit was conducted. Occupants of the 112 Jefferson Avenue location informed the Department they had no knowledge of Christians of Faith Academy. Because the school could not be located and student attendance could not be verified, the Department will not include Christians of Faith Academy with the published list of non-Chartered, non-tax-supported schools for the 2018–19 school year."

Shortly after, COF Academy's scheduled game against IMG Academy was canceled. Johnson's meetup with the premier high school football program in the country would have to wait. He and Hall were shocked. On October 17, Johnson sent an email to Angie Lawler, director of officiating and sport management for the OHSAA, asking for more information about the organization's decision, which had been announced weeks prior. "What changed in the information I gave you that would make us not a school. [*sic*] I thought we reported the information that you required. Did you need transcripts or anything? Did I forget to do something? Secondly, did someone send a letter/email letting us no [*sic*] why that decision was made? Is that possible so I can have it for our records?"

Lawler replied that there had been "multiple factors that led to our office's decision to rule COF Academy as a non-rated football team with regard to the Harbin computer ratings," and explained that the issue was less about "what changed" and more about a lack of information and a lack of communication from Johnson. She clarified that her department made multiple attempts to corroborate the information he provided, but said they were unable to do so. She even specified that Beau Rugg, OHSAA senior director of officiating and sport management at the time, had made efforts to call Johnson's cell phone directly, but was met with no reply and a full voicemail box. Johnson pressed Lawler for more details on how exactly the OHSAA "corroborated information" and wanted to meet with Rugg personally.

Hall bristled at what he felt was an incomplete investigation. He emailed Lawler, saying "So one attempt to contact Roy Johnson, instead of reaching out to a list of multiple individuals was how you 'corroborated' your information? And if in fact there were a multitude of attempts by phone, perhaps communication via email, with Roy Johnson, or anyone else … [that] would have been a more thorough and efficient way of gathering information, allowing you all to make a much more thought-out final decision?"

Rugg replied directly, sorry that he had ever agreed to consider granting COF Academy recognition in the first place. "I need to say that I was incorrect in originally agreeing that COF Academy would count in the Harbin Ratings. There was a timing issue and I should have waited a year to see the Academy become established. Our priority will always be to our member schools. I also need to say that I am very disturbed that you would send a sarcastic email to my staff. I don't usually sugarcoat things."

The final email in the exchange came from Hall. "Please don't be disturbed. Disturbing is when people's opinions of your institution become negatively skewed because OHSAA, an organization whose primary objective is to govern high school sports, tells an overzealous media constituent that 'COF Academy is no longer recognized as a school....' Especially when prior conversations led us to believe otherwise, not to mention the fact the Ohio Department of Education DOES consider COF Academy an Academic Institution. Surely, you can understand my disdain." The email from Hall—which claimed the ODE considered COF Academy a school days after the ODE had publicly stated they were not a school—was the final confirmation for the OHSAA. They could not trust the people running COF Academy.

By September, the AME Church Third District's stance on COF Academy had transitioned from quiet removal to outright denial. "[The AME Church] was never affiliated with them," church attorney Arthur Harmon said definitively at the time. "The persons that were involved in this, I believe, may be AME members of a local church or something like that. But they have gone off into their own business enterprise and, naturally, wanted to present their business enterprise to the AME Church and its members to see if they would be interested in that. If there was any representation that there was an affiliation or that the AME Church or the Third District was approving or disapproving of any of their actions, then that's not the case. There is no affiliation."

Those denials, however, only added more mystery to the situation. If the church hadn't been involved, where was the COF Academy unveiling event held? If no church officials had been working with Johnson, who did Egan and Kellam speak with? Those are questions the church was never able to answer, and Johnson provided a paper trail that kept the questions coming. He presented a $100,000 check dated December 18, 2015, that was deposited into a UBS bank account. The check didn't explicitly say anything about COF Academy or the Richard Allen Group, but the account number that appeared on the check matched other bank documents Johnson provided. The check was signed by Bishop McKinley Young and Third District accountant Floyd Alexander. "[Young] never authorized that check to go to the Richard Allen Group," Harmon said at the time. "That's what he told me. And I believe him."

Four months later, on March 10, 2016, Rev. Thompson, an AME Church pastor and assistant district accountant, emailed a UBS representative and carbon-copied Johnson. "As per our conversation, please provide me with the current statement on our account for the Richard Allen Group," read the email. Johnson also provided a letter written by Rev. Thompson two years later. Dated July 21, 2018, the letter was addressed to Dave Whinham, president and CEO of The Team LLC, a sports, media, and consulting company. The letter was sent on the AME Church Third Episcopal District letterhead, with Young's name included. In an email to Johnson the same day, Rev. Thompson wrote, "I am sending this letter to you. Please deliver to Mr. Whinham."

"It was good meeting with you yesterday! Thank you for the opportunity!" the letter begins. "As per our conversation, we are excited about the Christians of Faith Academy and look forward to your participation." The letter explains the church's background and elaborates on its "7,000 churches in 39 countries." It also mentions Johnson, Jay Richardson, and the Richard Allen Group. "We are also concerned about economic development and thus about six years ago, we created an economic-development arm for our work, the Richard Allen Group, a for-profit arm. It is the Richard Allen Group that is spearheading our development of the academy. Roy Johnson and Jay Richardson [are] authorized to assemble a team of persons and resources to bring this to fruition." The letter ends with a Bible verse, saying the project will "be investing in the future of our young people" and inviting

Whinham to "join us in this endeavor." Whinham didn't remember the specifics, but said he recalled having conversations with Johnson and Rev. Thompson.

In January of 2019, Rev. Thompson claimed he had no involvement with COF Academy or the Richard Allen Group, who were operating "independent of the church." He did acknowledge that Whinham's name sounded familiar, and answered as if he had been aware of the project. "We were supportive of the idea, as we have been with several other schools and educational training programs in our local and national community," he said. He claimed the check had been meant for a "money-market investment account" and he had no idea how it went to the Richard Allen Group. "How it got into what became their account, we have not been informed of," he said. "We've turned that in to the legal counsel." At that point, Rev. Thompson claimed he couldn't answer any more questions "because of the mess that's been created through this whole process" and hung up the phone. It was the last time he could be reached for comment.

After months of silence, even Richardson began talking about the church's connection to the project, though he did so out of an odd sense of honor. "I said [to Johnson], 'I can't let you be the fall guy,'" Richardson said at the time. Suddenly, Richardson wasn't as eager to definitively state that he wasn't involved with COF Academy, and he expressed rage at seeing the church's statement online. "I was like, 'Don't just take [the post] down. You have to make a statement saying there was a mistake made and apologize,'" he said at the time. "I don't think they understand the ramifications of a school, a football team, all that stuff being started under the pretense that this was backed and supported and endorsed by a faith-based entity. Everyone feels good about that. And then one day that faith-based entity wakes up and decides, 'No, we didn't have anything to do with that.' All the support left. All the funding left. All the sponsorships."

There were other signs of involvement between the church and Johnson, too. One email Johnson provided from 2017 showed that he and the Richard Allen Group were asked to help increase the efficiency of the Third District's buildings. To that end, Rev. Thompson sent Johnson energy information for the district's buildings and information from an energy-efficiency questionnaire. Later that year, Rev. Thompson discussed funding options for land planned to house COF Academy with members of the Prospera Advisory Group. He even emailed a "point of clarification" to specify that the project was expected to cost $3.1 million, which "includes the church, the annex, and the office building." Johnson was carbon-copied.

Johnson even provided an email chain between himself, Richardson, Rev. Thompson, and a "commercial relationship manager" at Huntington Bank that included a long discussion about loans for the COF Academy project. At one point, Rev. Thompson sent a variety of financial information that included boasting about the district's "160 churches in West Virginia, western Pennsylvania, and Ohio" and an explanation that those churches represent a gross income of $14.5 million and property value totaling $458 million.

When asked about those documents, Harmon simply reiterated that the church is not affiliated with Johnson, Richardson, or the Richard Allen Group. Instead, Harmon threw Rev. Thompson under the bus, presenting the theory that he had been working with Johnson without the church's knowledge. "Taylor Thompson may have been working with the Richard Allen Group," he said. "I still haven't nailed that one down yet. I think maybe he was." Young never publicly defended himself or the church, and on January 16, 2019, he died in Atlanta.

At one juncture in early 2019, Johnson repeatedly said he and his lawyers were considering pursuing legal action against the church. He claimed that he didn't want to rock the boat or to make things worse for the kids involved, and maintained at the time that he only wanted the church to keep their promises. "The only thing I think we really want them to do is just complete what you said you were going to do. Make sure the HER [Realtors] offices run okay. Make sure people have access to getting homes and good homes and understanding the buying process and that part of it. Make sure you continue to have something for the future and the next generation. Make sure people are aware that they can leave life insurance to their church and these community organizations. And lastly, help fund the school and do what you said you wanted to do by funding the school and make sure kids have a safe haven to go to school and use all their talents.... Give them an opportunity to have a shot at life itself."

What did he want out of a lawsuit? That was more difficult to say. Johnson considers himself a victim, but also often says that the children were the ones who were most damaged by the situation. "When you talk about lawsuits, you're talking about a lawsuit that just takes care of that, and I don't know if there's a number for that. Hopefully you can just talk about it with new leadership coming in, you can speak to new leadership and say, 'Hey, look, these are the things we wanted to do.' More importantly, if this is a money thing, 'This is how we plan to fund that.' So now you can fund this project and you can work and help kids. I mean, you're talking about a $7 million asset that was given. That's the part that confused federal investigators."

Johnson never filed a lawsuit against the church.

By early 2019, Johnson's problems had multiplied. He had become entangled in a variety of legal cases ranging in severity from unpaid car loans to fraud cases involving hundreds of thousands of dollars. But the real surprise came when the Secret Service came calling. He said the church's denial "led to an investigation and me being contacted by the feds to see if the school was legitimate, if the project was legitimate, and if the people who came and donated their time and funds and resources weren't defrauded and that it was a legitimate project."

He said in 2019 that investigators "found out that the project was legit" and simply "gathered information and closed the case, and that was about it." He said investigators told him they weren't investigating him or the church specifically, but were instead looking into the mysterious circumstances around the lack of a final product from all the planning that had been done. "They were investigating the fact that we opened a school and said we were a school and we had people come in and give money to knock down trees and all that. That's what they were investigating, because you can't go around and get Jeff Kellam to come in and do half a million dollars of work, CT Engineering to come in and donate $200,000 worth of work, can't get Mike Egan to come in and donate $100,000 of work … and most importantly I can't go to New Salem to say, 'Donate me a $7 million piece of land to build a school' if I wasn't going to build a school. That was never the case, so they were investigating that because someone said we weren't real or it was a fraud. If I did that, I'd be in jail."

Years later, he would say he's not a fan of talking about that particular speed bump. "I'm not talking about the Secret Service, so just stop," he said, referencing the many reporters who had asked him about it. "I'm not going to talk about it. The Secret Service brought me in. We cool. They cool. We on the same page. They ain't got a problem with me. I don't got a problem with them. And that's it."

Johnson and Richardson both said federal investigators interviewed them in late 2018 and early 2019. And in late November, a Gahanna Division of Police detective accidentally revealed that the investigation was taking place. Contacted by phone, she said she was looking into a complaint against Johnson and the Richard Allen Group and referenced a federal investigation being conducted by the Secret Service. Johnson claimed at the time that investigators were mainly interested in the time, resources, and land allegedly donated to the project.

No cathartic resolution would ever come for Johnson. The church stopped talking about the issue, and Young's death meant that one of the main people able to corroborate his story could never speak about it. Rev. Thompson has avoided speaking on the matter. And after years of wondering "Why would you leave $12 million on the table?" Johnson still doesn't know why the church cut ties with him, and he's still mad about it.

"I think they're all pieces of shit," he said. "And this is coming from someone who lies. I'm more deceitful than I am an outright liar. I don't necessarily lie, I just don't tell you the whole truth. I dance around the subject, all those deceitful things, which isn't any better. But [the church] after a bunch of financial institutions all saw these presentations, said, 'I have no idea who the Richard Allen Group is.' And then took it one step further and started telling banks, calling people and calling schools to tell them you had nothing to do with it. You started doing stuff that was causing issues all along, meanwhile in the back rooms where we're meeting, you're saying, 'It's okay. It's okay.'"

But that betrayal—and the loss of the church's money, sway, and assistance—didn't mark the end of Johnson's football dreams. In fact, his project was yet to hit its peak.

8

WE'LL SQUARE UP AT THE END

From nearly the moment COF Academy launched, civil lawsuits and criminal allegations followed.

Most people would lose sleep over the fear of lawsuits and nights in jail, but Johnson was accustomed to the workings of the American court system, and had perfected a variety of methods of exploiting the weaknesses of that system. Namely, for any lawsuit to begin, criminal or civil, the accused must first be found and served a subpoena with the general allegations. Johnson frequently took advantage of his uncanny ability to duck these papers, meaning many lawsuits never got off the ground. And that practice wasn't unique to COF Academy or Bishop Sycamore; Johnson had made a habit of ignoring court orders.

Ranging from offenses as minor as a parking ticket to as major as domestic violence, Johnson has had a warrant issued for his arrest or a summons for his appearance in court at least 42 documented times. To account for all of the money Johnson owes various individuals, businesses, or government entities would be a book of its own, and would include multiple shell companies and schemes that predate his football coaching career. But even focusing solely on the matters of COF Academy and Bishop Sycamore, the lawsuits quickly pile up.

Much of the work for COF Academy was done through the Richard Allen Group. Lawsuits against the company shed light into how far Johnson was willing to go in order to avoid consequences for his actions.

In August of 2018, Heartland Bank filed a lawsuit against Johnson, Richardson, and RAG just as COF Academy's first season was getting underway. The lawsuit stated that in February of 2018, a loan for $92,020 had been taken out by Richardson and Johnson under their company name. Payments on the loan stopped soon after, leaving an outstanding balance of $90,499.10. An attorney for RAG confessed that the company did owe the money and did not fight the judgment in court. But what looked to be an open-and-shut case revealed a confusing labyrinth that would complicate matters when Heartland Bank tried to secure repayment on the loan.

All bank accounts associated with RAG were empty, according to the banks subpoenaed in the court case. To get their money back, Heartland Bank got a court order to repossess a 2017 Range Rover that was purchased by RAG. But, according to court documents, the organization "had relocated the vehicle, closed operations, was no longer at any of the address[es] provided at the time of signing the Note, and failed to respond to all inquiries of Heartland Bank as to the location of the vehicle … Heartland Bank discovered that

TRAG had transferred the Ohio Certificate of Title to the Vehicle free of any liens, without the permission or approval of Heartland, to Leroy Johnson Jr. Mr. Johnson Jr. failed to respond to all inquiries as to the location of the Vehicle until January of 2019, when, at the direction of law enforcement in an unrelated matter, he was instructed to provide Heartland Bank with the Vehicle's location."

Despite being forced to reveal the vehicle's location, Johnson continued to hold up the process by refusing to sign over the title of the Range Rover or provide the keys to it. Johnson simply dropped the vehicle off at the Heartland Bank location in Whitehall, Ohio, and left it there with no means to access it. A court order had to be obtained for a new title, and the estimated $60,000 value of the vehicle did not cover the full outstanding balance of the loan, which had yet to be repaid by either Johnson or Richardson. Still, Heartland Bank was able to recoup some funds. That is more than can be said for most of Johnson's victims.

Bob Van Horn has been an Ohio High School Athletics Association official in eight sports for over three decades. He's officiated for other organizations for more than 50 years total. In 2018, he was contacted by Roy Johnson to officiate one of COF Academy's home games. The fee for the crew was $350. "An assigner had called me up and asked me if I was interested in doing the game," Van Horn recalled. "I said, 'Yeah,' and he said, 'Now, it's not through Ohio High School,' because they were denied acceptance, and 'I've had some issues in the past with them being slow to pay, so get your money the night of the game.' I had no problem with that. Before the game, Van Horn asked Johnson if he could be paid, as they agreed to. Johnson, who told Van Horn he was the school's athletic director, balked, claiming he didn't have his checkbook on him. He claimed he'd find Van Horn at halftime. "I recognized this wasn't good right away." Johnson never showed up, and when Van Horn approached head coach Paul Williams asking about payment, Williams wasn't able to provide payment either.

"Two of the [officials] basically said, 'We aren't going to get paid, we're leaving,'" Van Horn said, "I gave them cash so they were covered. Doing the game is the priority. After the game of course there's nobody there, can't find anybody. I flagged Roy Johnson down and said, 'Hey, we didn't get paid before the game, we didn't get paid at half time, and now it's after the game, what's going on?' And he said, 'Is it okay if we pay you in cash?' I said sure, and he asked to meet on Wednesday. And that's the last time I ever spoke to him. I left messages for six months and never got paid."

Van Horn tried to recoup what he had lost in small claims court, but Johnson was never officially served papers in the lawsuit, which was also filed against the AME Church, the Richard Allen Group, and COF Academy. Default judgment was granted to Van Horn, and he has a lien against RAG but has never been paid. "Our not getting paid is bad enough, but to use the Tammy Faye routine of bilking people in the name of religion, that's just one thing I can't stomach," Van Horn said. "In over 50 years of officiating, it's the only time I've ever been stiffed." In addition to not receiving the game fee, Van Horn also is out the $78 he paid to file the lawsuit in small claims court.

In addition to his inclusion in a long and continuously growing list of lawsuits, some of Johnson's victims never took him to court at all. Such was the case with Dave Pando, owner of LVL UP Sports Paintball Park in Grove City, Ohio. In 2018, during the COF Academy season, Johnson took the football team to the park for a team-building day in the middle of the week.

"I was at the paintball park and I got a call from Roy Johnson saying, 'Hey, I've got a busload of kids, we were supposed to play paintball somewhere and they couldn't get us in, so we were hoping you could do a last-minute paintball outing for me and 40 kids.' He told me they were underprivileged kids and asked if I could hook them up and get them in today," Pando said. "We were a new, small business at the time, and my philosophy was always to get as many people here to play as possible, even at a discount, just to get our name out there. So of course I said yes and scrambled a staff together to host this group—40 people is a lot for one group at a paintball park. I gave them a big discount—about half the price of what I'd normally charge—because I wanted to take care of the kids and he told me they were underprivileged and I knew that budget would be an issue. Because it was all last-minute, I didn't take a deposit. I told them to just show up and we'd figure it out. I usually trust people. The kids had a blast. Kids love paintball, and we made it pretty easy for them to have a great time."

Johnson talked to Pando during the outing, and like most people, Pando was charmed by him. The two men discussed the background of the program, the kids who were involved, and the goals that Johnson had. Now, Pando sees him as a "con artist." But in retrospect, he doesn't know how he could have expected what was coming after the conversation they had. "He was very nice. I thought he was super genuine and he pulled on my heartstrings when he was explaining how desperate he was to have this party. In most circumstances, it would be very tough for me to put together a staff to host a 40-person paintball group on a weekday when we're not normally open. He basically said, 'These kids really want to play football; they're really good kids who are from bad parent situations.' I believed the crap out of him. I really wanted to help these kids. We have the opportunity to help underprivileged kids, and that's what paintball is good for. It's the service we bring to our community: a good place for families and teens and anyone else. So what he was asking was right up our alley and I wanted to help him. He was very genuine and convincing. And I guess, aside from the money, he wasn't really lying about the situation. The only thing he didn't mention to me was that he wasn't going to pay me. He was sweet. I liked him."

At one point, Johnson handed him a credit card, saying, "Just hang on to this and we'll square up at the end." He told Pando he might have to leave early, and if that happened, Pando could simply charge the credit card and Johnson would come back to pick it up another day. That's relatively common for Pando to hear, so he thought nothing of it.

"When the bus left, I swiped the card and it was declined. I assumed because it was for a maximum charge situation. I called him and he didn't answer, so I started to get concerned. I called him from another number and he answered and said, 'I'm so sorry the credit card didn't work. What time do you close? I'll be by there with a check for the full amount.' Of course he never showed up and never answered my phone calls again after that."

Pando never filed a lawsuit or called police to try and recoup his expenses from the theft, and instead tried to find a way to get Johnson to accept responsibility for the charges, which he estimated was around $1,000.

"I was obsessed with this. It was the first time we had been screwed over really bad since we opened, and I was pissed. I went out of my way to put this together for these guys and gave them a discount and everything else. That meant a lot to us back then. It made a huge difference as a small business with a ton of debt trying to make it past the three-year mark and survive. And it pissed me off because you trust that people are going to do the right thing and then you just get burned." Pando called Johnson repeatedly, using different phone numbers and calling at various times of the day. He even began messaging Johnson and other COF Academy coaches and players on social media, trying to get anyone to respond.

"I'm trying to make him mad, I'm calling so much. The kids almost seemed embarrassed. They felt bad and said, 'I'm so sorry, I'll talk to Roy,'" Pando said. Eventually, Johnson answered the phone. "I called him out and he gives me this big guilt trip story about how they're waiting on some money to clear and something about the church. It was a bunch of bullshit about how he couldn't pay, but he promised me he would give me a check in the next three days. That was the last time I ever heard from him. I still have his credit card in the cash register."

Pando didn't see any red flags or perceive any warning signs from Johnson on the day of the event. The story seemed sincere enough, and Pando believes in the ability of paintball to serve as a community builder. "I would describe him as a con artist," Pando said. "He knew when he walked in here that he didn't have that church money. His story that he told me was that it was coming and it just never came."

Pando continued to try and get the money he was owed, going so far as to call the AME Church. "Whoever I talked to, I must not have been the first person to do this because she immediately said, 'We are not affiliated with that guy. Do not call here again.' She basically yelled at me, like she was annoyed I was calling about that. I could tell I wasn't the first person to follow the breadcrumbs and call her."

And even though Pando never received repayment for the day of paintball, while "doing his own detective work" on the case, he came into contact with Deryck Richardson, who sympathized with Pando's situation and has since become a repeat customer of his business.

Few have put in as much work in trying to reclaim what they've lost as Pando, but his story is sadly not unique. SuperKick Columbus, the facility in which COF Academy occasionally practiced and held its odd media day, was never paid, leaving a total bill of $7,720. Like many others before him, owner and CEO Jim Waters was swayed into delusion by talk of admirable goals and helping the disadvantaged youth. He said his organization was "guilty of not following our usual processes" because of the pitch by Johnson and a "long line of correspondence" that Waters called lies. "A consistent theme about this is that Roy is very convincing with the purpose of the school and the story and all of that," he said in 2018. "They took advantage of our goodwill under the guise of charity."

Johnson's non-payment of debts continued when Bishop Sycamore began. In March of 2021, Cardinal Transportation filed a lawsuit claiming that Johnson and Andre Peterson hired the company to provide transportation to football games. Johnson and Peterson used a company name, "ISE Foundation." According to the lawsuit, they racked up nearly $13,000 in charges and never paid any amount toward that debt. The main issue? The ISE Foundation did not exist. This made Johnson and Peterson personally liable for the debt. However, Johnson was never found to officially serve papers to, meaning the case never advanced. It was dismissed due to the inability to find Johnson in May of 2022.

This wasn't the first time the nonexistent ISE Foundation was used to try and limit personal liability. In September of 2020, Peterson and Johnson, along with dozens of players, were evicted from The Commons on Kinnear, an apartment complex in Columbus. All of the apartments had been rented under the players' names, and jointly under the name of the ISE Foundation. In total, 37 players were named as defendants in the eviction cases. Additionally, 10 John and Jane Does were named as defendants. They were residents of the apartments under the ISE Foundation name, but the complex was never able to find their real names. Of the 37 named individuals, not every person could be identified. Some names could simply have been misspelled, while others may be fictitious altogether. All named parties avoided being served papers in the lawsuit, so the money owed was never repaid.

Evictions were commonplace for Johnson. He and the players under his care were evicted from the Griff apartments and from the Bryden Road apartments in 2019. In COF Academy's very first game against Football North, a team from Canada, Johnson agreed to pay for the hotel room for the visiting team as well as his own. Everyone stayed at a Baymont Inn. None of the rooms were paid for, leaving a debt of $110,685. Johnson avoided service on the lawsuit that would follow the unpaid bill, and the money was never repaid.

At the end of Johnson's run as a football administrator, after what would become the infamous IMG Academy game, a criminal investigation was opened when Johnson attempted to pay for the hotel rooms at the Fairfield Inn and Suites by Marriott Canton South with invalid checks. Johnson rented 25 rooms, amassing a total charge of $3,596. No charges were ever filed in the criminal investigation, and the debt was never paid.

On August 16, 2021, three days before the first game of Bishop Sycamore's season, Johnson took the team to eat at BD's Mongolian Grill in Columbus. According to a police report filed in September of that year, "complainant reported that suspect left his restaurant without paying for a significant amount of food ordered for himself and his football team. Complainant stated that the team came into the restaurant and suspect asked the staff if they 'accepted school checks' which complainant agreed to accept. Prior to leaving, suspect stated that he had to 'text someone else to bring the check.' Complainant stated that suspect then left the restaurant with the remainder of his team and the bill was never paid." The bill totaled $518. No arrests were ever made, and a spokesperson for the Columbus Division of Police said the case is currently inactive. Johnson would later brag about taking the team to Mongolian Barbecue as support for the claim that he fed his players properly.

In court, Johnson's strategy is often to not fight the allegations against him. He simply avoids court altogether, thus avoiding paying the fines or debt. It's a method that's proven successful for him. After learning from the Heartland Bank case, Johnson avoided having anything legally in his name. With no car titles, mortgages, or bank accounts to seize, there is no way to satisfy the debt. Johnson either does not work or hides his employment, leaving no paycheck for the victims to garnish. Even in his personal life, Johnson uses this technique. In August of 2021, a lawsuit was filed by HS Financial Group against Johnson after he leased a table from Payless Furniture and bounced three checks made out as the payment, leaving a debt of nearly $1,400. However, when the company went to repossess the furniture, they couldn't find Johnson or the table. The debt has not been repaid.

This strategy has since been mirrored by his partners, with various amounts of success. Peterson would hire an attorney named Josiah Collier to represent him and the Bishop Sycamore Foundation in the eviction case from the Bryden Road apartments. The eviction still occurred, and it produced a second lawsuit—this time from Collier. Peterson never paid the attorney his $1,200 fee. The attorney hired to fight a case about non-payment found himself not getting paid. Collier was unable to ever serve the papers on Peterson, and the court case was eventually dismissed without Collier recouping any money.

These are just some of the many people and businesses that Johnson, Richardson, and Peterson did not pay. It's unlikely all victims will ever be known, given how frequent the fraud was.

And while Johnson and his associates managed to wiggle out of a stunning number of cases, one institution is using every technique possible to get their money back in a court case that is still ongoing. First Merchants Bank, headquartered in Muncie, Indiana, has been fighting Johnson, Richardson, and RAG in court for more than four years to recoup funds from a $100,000 loan, of which not a dime has ever been paid.

The lawsuit began on November 26, 2018, shortly after the conclusion of COF Academy's football season. The complaint accuses Johnson and Richardson of a litany of misdeeds, including fraud, forgery, and passing bad checks. According to the lawsuit, Richardson and Johnson told the bank that they were the president and secretary of the Third Episcopal District of the African Methodist Episcopal Church in Columbus, and that the loan was for the church. The bank extended them a loan on April 23, 2018, and after it was granted, it immediately went into default. No payments were ever made. The lawsuit reads, "upon the occurrence of the default, [First Merchants Bank] began investigation the default, and, among other things, communicated and met with the Church, inclusive of Reverend Dr. Taylor T. Thompson, regarding the loan and the default. During those communications and meeting, Rev. Thompson indicated that the Church had no knowledge of the loan, was not a party thereto, and did not receive any proceeds or benefits from the loan."

When presented with a letter that was purported to bear his signature, Rev. Thompson claimed it was a forgery and that information used by Johnson and Richardson to obtain the loan was false. The signature on the loan application does not match a letter provided by Johnson in 2018 that also purports to bear Rev. Thompson's signature. The only time a payment was attempted on the loan was in September of 2018. Johnson provided the bank with a $7,000 check that bounced. The bank argued this was an attempt to defraud them and delay default proceedings because Johnson "knew the [check] would be dishonored."

The first hurdle for the bank was the same hurdle all other lawsuits against Johnson faced—they had to find him. The bank sent subpoenas to multiple addresses and even went as far as to hire a process server to attempt to locate Johnson and Richardson so that they could serve the papers for the lawsuit. They were not successful. It wasn't until February of 2019 that the lawsuit began, thanks to Johnson and Richardson filing paperwork with the court stating they would be representing themselves in the lawsuit. They denied the claims against them, and also tried to file to represent the Richard Allen Group. But since Johnson and Richardson are not attorneys, they could not legally represent their company in the case. A status conference was set for April 2 to begin the legal process. Johnson and Richardson did not appear.

A new conference was set for April 9, this time including a threat. If Johnson and Richardson did not appear to this date, they could be held in contempt of court, with a default judgment entered against them. This would mean the court would rule in favor of the bank on all counts. With such a heavy penalty for non-compliance, Johnson and Richardson made sure to attend. They also hired two attorneys to represent RAG, Christopher O'Shaughnessy and Teresa Hardymon of the firm Hahn Loeser & Parks. The attorneys' first move was to ask the court to add a new defendant to the case, The AME Church.

According to a filing from RAG, it was the Church who benefitted from the loan agreement, not Johnson and Richardson. They stated once again that RAG is the financial arm of the church, with Richardson being the president of RAG and Johnson the secretary. They claimed RAG were "authorized to act on behalf of the Church and did so with Bishop McKinley Young's and Rev. Thompson's knowledge and authorization." Further, they claimed that Rev. Thompson was present at the time the loan was signed. As evidence of their claims, they provided a document stating that RAG was the financial arm of the church, purportedly signed by Johnson, Richardson, and Rev. Thompson. The letter was undated.

The bank denied these claims. They said, "The [church] did not enter into any agreement, written or oral, to subsidize, fund, finance, or guarantee any action, effort, or adventure of the Richard Allen Group or any of the Defendants

[Johnson and Richardson]. The Richard Allen Group is not the financial arm of the [church] ... Mr. Johnson and Mr. Richardson have engaged in a course of fraudulent conduct by convincing the [Bank] that they were part of and represented the [church]." The church further said they never received any of the proceeds of the loan, in contrast to the claims of Johnson and Richardson.

The following months were filled with various court filings and arguments on matters of policy and proceedings between the church, Johnson, Richardson, and RAG. The next major change came in July of 2020, when RAG's lawyers withdrew from the case. The company was again without representation. There was no reason given as to why, after over a year of representing RAG, the law firm was stepping away. No one else was hired to fill the void.

Johnson and Rev. Thompson both sat for depositions in August of 2020. After that, the bank felt they had all the evidence needed to end the case, and filed a motion for summary judgment in September. In Johnson's deposition, he admitted there was nothing in writing indicating that RAG was the financial arm of the Church. This was in direct conflict to the document Johnson himself produced as evidence earlier in the case. Johnson further admitted that the proceeds from the loan were deposited into a Huntington Bank account held by Mjolnir Development, a fictitious trade name for the

Richard Allen Group. The only person with access to that bank account was Johnson himself.

Following the depositions, the bank provided more written questions for Johnson, Richardson, and RAG to answer in court. With no lawyer, RAG had no one to answer the questions. Johnson and Richardson never did. When questions aren't answered within 28 days of filing, the court finds the claims as factual by default. As such, the following statements were taken as fact, pursuant to Johnson's deposition and lack of claims to the contrary:

- The AME Church never authorized or approved TRAG to serve as their financial arm.
- Johnson and Richardson were never authorized to obtain the loan from the Bank.
- The information provided by Johnson and Richardson to obtain the loan was false.
- All of the money from the loan went to either TRAG or Johnson himself.

Despite not answering the questions posed by the bank in court filings, Johnson and Richardson filed a motion against the summary judgment request in November of 2020. They argued that although they couldn't prove the Church authorized RAG to act as their financial arm in any way, and although RAG obtained all of the proceeds from the loan, a verbal agreement did exist and, as such, RAG, Johnson, and Richardson should not be liable. At the very least, they argued, the matter should proceed to a trial, and that once the loan was issued, it was the property of the church. If the loan proceeds went missing or were unpaid, Johnson argued, only the church could sue him, not the bank.

The court was unconvinced by Johnson's last-ditch arguments. Summary judgment was awarded to the bank on all claims except for the claim of the bad check, as the judge determined there was enough evidence to proceed to trial on that claim. The bank dropped the charge of the bad check, not wanting to expend more resources to recoup an extra $7,000 when it had just won a claim of over $100,000. In his decision, the judge stated that due to RAG, Richardson, and Johnson failing to properly respond to the bank's requests for admissions, they were taken as true. With those statements being accepted as true by the court, the case was settled. But the story doesn't end there. A damages hearing was held in January of 2022 to determine the final amount owed to the bank after interest and court costs.

There were very few surprises in the hearing to award damages because the issue of guilt had already been decided by default, as Johnson, Richardson, and the Richard Allen Group had not provided answers to the court in a timely manner. That fact appeared to elude the two men, however, who represented themselves in the case. At the beginning of the hearing, the magistrate in charge of the proceeding explicitly said, "To make it very clear, in case there is any doubt, the judge has already ruled that First Merchants Bank is entitled to a judgment against the two of you and the LLC. The only issue is the amount of damages to be awarded ultimately when that final judgment is entered. The evidence this morning that I expect First Merchants Bank to present is on the issue of dollars, and any other associated damages that they might be seeking, not the issue of whether or not the judgment is appropriate. I just wanted to tell you that up front that we're not going to get into that issue, in case you might be anticipating there being evidence on the issue of whether or not a judgment should be taken against you, that issue has already been ruled upon."

When asked if he wanted to make an opening statement, Richardson's first question was to the point the magistrate just covered. "I don't have an opening statement at this point, I just wanted to clarify that we are past the point of discussing liability, is that correct?" The magistrate affirmed it was. Johnson did not make an opening statement. The bank called only one witness, first vice president and director of special assets David Hunt, who testified about the loan documentation and the amount that Johnson and Richardson were liable for.

Richardson chose not to cross examine Hunt, but Johnson did take the opportunity. He asked Hunt, "Are you aware of the relationship between myself and Mr. Richardson and the AME Church? What is your understanding of that relationship?" The bank's lawyer objected, saying that the information had nothing to do with the amount of damages. The magistrate asked Johnson to explain how the question was relevant to the issue of the amount of damages owed. Johnson answered, "To me it's relevant because I just want to find out what he knows about the whole situation." The magistrate sustained the objection and did not allow the question to be answered. Johnson continued with multiple other questions relating to assets and collateral, all of which were disallowed by the magistrate, who only allowed a few questions regarding interest and late fees before shutting down Johnson's final question. "Based off the information, and again, you're looking at all the files and everything else, do you feel like First Merchants was frauded by myself?"

The magistrate quickly clarified, "The judge has already ruled on that issue, and he did rule affirmatively that there was fraud."

Johnson didn't want to let the issue go, asking one further time, "Do you agree with that?"

"That's not relevant," was the magistrate's curt reply.

A resigned Johnson said, "My man, I appreciate you," and ended his questioning.

When it came time to end the hearing and accept the original loan documents as evidence, Richardson attempted a last-minute objection. "I object to all the documents on the grounds that my signature is not on them, but I know that's not what we're here for," Richardson said. The magistrate noted the objection, and overruled it.

The amount was set at $120,602.09, with interest still accruing. Despite the facts being settled from a legal standpoint, the hardest portion still remained—finding and recouping the money. In October 2022, the bank filed a motion to force both men to answer, under oath, about their income and financial holdings so that the bank could seize whatever assets they may have to satisfy the loan. Johnson and Richardson both skipped the hearing. Payments have begun to be made on the loan through garnishments of Richardson's paycheck from Sinclair Broadcasting, the owner of WSYX ABC6 in Columbus. Twenty-five percent of each payment Richardson receives goes towards the debt, but Johnson only makes roughly $19,000 a year. At that rate, it would take around 25 years for the loan to be repaid. The bank continues to try to find what other sources of income Johnson and Richardson have, and they have filed a motion to have both men held in contempt of court for failing to disclose that information. The motion has not yet been ruled on.

In their ongoing attempts to recoup some of their seemingly lost funds, First Merchants Bank tried one final avenue: a lawsuit against SMAC Entertainment. SMAC was the production company who was, in 2022, in the process of making a Bishop Sycamore documentary. One of the largest challenges facing the bank in their quest to recoup their funds was Johnson's lack of clear income. So when the bank learned that SMAC had paid Johnson for the rights to his life story, they saw an opportunity. Because Johnson did not have "sufficient real or personal property" to satisfy his debts, the bank argued that any money SMAC was due to send Johnson should instead go to the bank. This time, Johnson would not be able to successfully dodge the court papers, allowing for the rare instance of the matter proceeding swiftly. Johnson did not file any arguments with the court to allege that he should be able to keep the money, and default judgment was granted to the bank. First Merchants Bank is now "entitled to payments due and owing to Johnson now or in the future" that come as a result of his contract with SMAC entertainment.

Still, the legal right to the payment is only half the battle. The other half of that battle will be to collect the payment, a step that has eluded the bank for the length of their legal fight. So, in an attempt to try and cut out Johnson himself as a middleman in the transaction, First Merchants Bank reached a deal with SMAC. The deal says that "SMAC Entertainment acknowledges that it has not paid any money to Defendant Johnson in connection with the HBO documentary regarding him. SMAC Entertainment acknowledges that it entered into an agreement ... as of November 8, 2021, with Defendant Johnson to option and acquire the exclusive rights to Defendant Johnson's life story in connection with a scripted project, and as of the date of this entry, it does not owe any money to Defendant Johnson ... by agreement of the parties, SMAC Entertainment shall pay or transfer to Plaintiff First Merchants Bank all monies or other considerations, if any, which would be paid now or anytime in the future to Defendant Johnson." If and when a movie is ever made about the Bishop Sycamore saga, Roy Johnson's cut will be headed straight to his creditors.

The most recent lawsuit to come out of the Bishop Sycamore scandal would come from the state of Ohio itself. In the fall of 2021, the Ohio Attorney General's Office began looking into the Bishop Sycamore Foundation, a nonprofit organization founded by Andre Peterson, presumably to handle the finances related to Bishop Sycamore. What the attorney general's office found was the same issue that always plagued Bishop Sycamore and COF Academy before it: unpaid debts. This time, those debts came as the result of unpaid wages.

In a letter to Peterson dated October 21, 2021, the Ohio Department of Commerce said the office "recently completed an investigation into the wages paid by your company. The audit revealed violations of Ohio's Minimum Wage Law, Chapter 4111, of the Ohio Revised Code and, as a result, it has been determined that back wages are owed. Attached please find a list of the employee(s) or former employee(s) and information showing the computations that resulted in this determination."

The only employee listed in the document is Nicholas Brobeck. The complaint is on behalf of an employee hired for unspecified work and was allegedly never paid. At the rate of minimum wage, the report says, he would have been owed $1,566.40. But the state also includes damages of $3,132.80 for a total amount owed of $4,699.20. The notice from the state does, however, provide Peterson with an avenue to avoid charges. "To correct this matter, you will need to forward a check to this office for each of the listed employee(s) or former employee(s)." No payment was ever received. Almost a year after the letter was sent, on September 22, 2022, the state of Ohio filed a lawsuit against Peterson and the Bishop Sycamore foundations to recoup the funds, with Peterson also on the hook for any attorney fees in the case.

9

THIS TIME, WE'RE GOING TO DO IT RIGHT

In spite of the spectacular and public manner of COF Academy's single-season failure, in early 2019—as Johnson fought his legal battles, spoke to the Secret Service, and attempted to fade into the background—an appetite remained for something that filled the role of that original plan: a school that could fill the gaps and help kids get to college.

At the time, Mike Egan, the extraordinarily overqualified developer at the heart of plans for COF Academy's conceptual campus, said he had been watching the program's downfall from afar and wished its initial goals could have been met. "What's crazy is that there's still a chance to do something," he said at the time. "I hate how it's come out, but the need is still there. There are people like myself who are willing to make it work." Jeff Kellam, owner of construction company Kellam Inc., felt the same way. "There are people in this world who could write out a check for $12 million or $1 million or $500,000. I still don't get why no one has stepped up and said, 'Here, let's keep it going. Here's a check.' It was, in my opinion, an excellent plan."

For those two men, the issue wasn't the failure of the football program—it was the kids and families abandoned along the way. "Anybody I talked to, I said, 'What about the kids? Has everybody forgotten about the kids? I thought this project was about the kids. What's going on with all this?'" Kellam said. "Everybody forgot about our informal promise to the kids." Egan had no idea what would happen next, but was hopeful that it would be something positive. "I don't know what's going to come out of it, but I hope that there will be some type of curing for people."

For Andre Peterson and his son, Javan Peterson, the only way to reach that cure would be to keep going.

A year before, Javan had been weighing the options for his sophomore year. He was in the process of enrolling at Reynoldsburg High School when COF Academy officials contacted him about what they were building. Like other players, the lineman said their promises of a bigger spotlight and college opportunities were attractive. "It was my idea to go to COF," he said. "[My parents] were asking, 'Javan, do you really want to go there or do you want to stay where you are?' I wanted to go because I felt like what the team had and the competition I could have on that level, it was better for me to start doing that."

Andre agreed that COF Academy presented an interesting option. The ordained minister and former youth and high school coach, who played collegiately at Youngstown State under famed coach Jim Tressel, spoke to Johnson and others involved, and jumped on board as a jack-of-all-trades organizer and coach. "I liked the concept of it," he said. "I'm a former [college] football player and I kind of wanted Javan to get the opportunity to play against some of the best competition—not just in Ohio but around the country. I liked what they showed me; I liked what I was hearing."

But as the season progressed, he watched as promises went unfulfilled. As one of the many families and staff members to help guide COF Academy students through the lack of living arrangements and meals, he confronted Johnson about the issues the program was having. At one point, he said Johnson finally took his guard down and admitted the challenges he was facing. It would be a bonding moment for the two men. "As me and him talked more and more, he kind of opened up more and more about what was going on and the concerns that he had as far as the financing when the church backed out," Andre said. "You always think, 'Is somebody trying to hustle you?' I didn't feel like it was a hustle."

Peterson grew increasingly more involved, and eventually found himself surprised with what Johnson and COF Academy were able to accomplish. "One of the main focuses that I look at in this situation are the young men we had playing and in school," he said. "I think it took a lot to recognize what was really going on with the church and realizing that Roy felt like he had to do this on his own. It took him reaching out to some people and some churches and some people in the community and some parents that donated their money and their time to make sure kids made it."

Entering the tumultuous world of Johnson and the COF Academy and Bishop Sycamore projects, Peterson was no stranger to financial worries. In 2014, he and his wife filed for bankruptcy after a series of lawsuits against them for unpaid debts. Peterson found himself on the wrong side of at least six lawsuits in Franklin County alone, ranging from unpaid medical debts to real estate issues. But that wasn't the most serious visit to a courtroom for Peterson. He was familiar with the legal system, having worked as a police officer in Youngstown in the 1990s. That career ended for Peterson after he resigned from the job amid being implicated in a murder investigation.

On August 9, 1998, Bradrick McMillan was shot in the head outside the Elks Club on Highland Avenue in Warren Township in northeast Ohio, just outside of Youngstown. McMillan was a police informant who planned on testifying against three individuals in a drug case: Shawn Armstrong, Lance Pough, and Art Bell. Bell and Pough pled guilty to the murder charge, and Armstrong was found guilty at trial. But the prosecutors admitted they were not sure who actually pulled the trigger of the gun that killed McMillan—a gun that belonged to Andre Peterson. The car that was driven to commit the murder that night also belonged to Peterson. In an interview with the *Youngstown Vindicator* published on September 21, 2001, Peterson denied any involvement with the murder. "I don't have anything to hide, I want to talk," Peterson said at the time, claiming that he and McMillan were friends and that he would not have taken part in his death.

Peterson took and passed a polygraph exam that included questions like whether he knew the murder was going to take place and if he willingly gave anyone his gun. Peterson could not answer why Armstrong had his car and weapon. He stated the gun must have been stolen, and reported it as such three days after the homicide. Prosecutors said that Armstrong was a friend of Peterson's and that he was living in Peterson's house at the time. Peterson was never charged in the case, and when called to testify in the murder trial of Armstrong, Peterson declined to do so, taking the Fifth Amendment right to not incriminate himself. His partner, Carlo Eggleston, was also never charged, despite Pough testifying that he had paid Eggleston $6,700 to commit the murder. The FBI helped investigate the case, and said that Peterson was not a suspect. Still, the incident cost him his job as a law enforcement officer. Armstrong was convicted in 2001, but was freed from jail in 2006. His conviction was overturned and the charges dismissed because of a lack of evidence of his guilt. Prosecutors did not retry the case.

After a tumultuous COF Academy season, Javan was happy with the choice he made. Unlike some other students, he and Andre said he continued to take classes through the Edmentum program, and had garnered interest from his dad's alma mater and been invited to a spring game at the University of Pittsburgh. He portrayed the year with the team in a much more positive light than others. "It was a good experience," he said. "For it being my first year playing [high school] football, I felt like I got a lot of lessons out of it."

Andre saw that too, and said that in spite of "the struggles" faced by the program, "it still worked out for the good for some of these kids." That taste of success—or at least of a positive influence on the lives of the students involved—made Peterson wonder what could come next for the students and staff that were left behind by the downfall of COF Academy. And he said the lessons he learned along the way had pushed him to launch a new school. He would call it Bishop Sycamore.

On January 19, 2019, BishopSycamore.org was registered. It was the first official foray into the new school, and for Andre, it represented the start of something new, and a chance to right the wrongs of the last idea. "I liked the concept of what Roy was trying to do," he said. "Me and some of the other parents and some of the people that were involved decided to continue that."

By August of 2019, the "Bishop Sycamore Foundation" had been registered as a nonprofit in Ohio, but by then Andre had been working on the project for some time. And he was extremely confident in their ability to learn from previous failures. "Every issue that COF had, we're doing what's necessary to not have that issue," he said. "One of the biggest things is we're not relying on one entity to supply us with our funding. We'll have a school building. We'll have teachers. It'll still be online with Edmentum, but some of those things are going to be different. That's how much I believe in that vision."

Bishop Sycamore would never have a school building or any teachers.

At the beginning of the project, Andre and Johnson both agreed that the face of COF Academy wouldn't be involved in Bishop Sycamore. Johnson said he helped Andre set up the website and answered some questions for him, but claimed his attorneys told him he "can't really be involved." For his part, Johnson said he had no interest. He was too tired.

It wouldn't take long, however, before the face of COF Academy became a key figure in Bishop Sycamore. "[Andre] asked me and I kept saying, 'I don't want to do this shit. I'm good.' I wasn't going to. My daughter was being born, the Secret Service was pulling me in. I was so done with this shit,"

Johnson said. "And then they had a meeting and I stopped by and saw half of my players there. They were like, 'I can't go back to my regular school. We need help.'" That was all the convincing he needed.

Soon, the same cast of characters from 2018 were experiencing déjà vu. "Pretty quickly, I started hearing things I had heard a year ago," Deryck Richardson said. "'Funding is coming; it's coming. Oh man, our funding fell through, how can we do this? I can't believe our investors backed out.' Those were things I had heard before. At that point, I told Roy that I was out and that he should shut this thing down until he got the funding." But that wasn't the kind of advice Johnson wanted to hear. "It's almost like he figured out, 'I can do this without funding.' I don't believe that he thought he'd start a school without funding. What I do believe is that there were funding opportunities and, for whatever reason, they fell through. When the investors backed out, Roy said, 'I did it once before without money. I guess we're here now.'"

Deryck had been here before, and knew that he needed to keep his name and his team further away from the project than he had with COF Academy. He would occasionally see Johnson around the office building they once shared, and after the COF Academy debacle, it always made him uncomfortable. "Even though the public didn't know who

Bishop Sycamore was, my guys certainly knew who Roy was. We were running two businesses out of there, and the offices are pretty close quarters. It's not like people don't know what's going on, so I didn't want the distraction of Roy coming in, and I felt that we got distracted by Roy and COF. I see that as a business deal gone bad. I didn't want to have my guys see that, because they knew it was a business deal gone bad too."

Defensive coordinator and recruiter Ulysses Hall had walked away from the COF Academy program on bad terms. He hadn't been paid what he was owed, and had upended his life to chase a project that he was never sure would be to his benefit anyway. Johnson knew that, and "went dark" with Hall for some time. But when the Bishop Sycamore plan began in earnest, Johnson called him anyway to attempt to convince him to return.

"He was like, 'Man, we've got to try. We're going to do it right, do it again.' I'm like, 'Bro, I'm not doing this again.'" Johnson tried to sway him. "'Even if we get it going first?'" he offered. But Hall wasn't interested at all. "My whole desire to even be a high school football coach is tainted."

In spite of the reunion of much of the COF Academy cast and crew, there's no indication that Jay Richardson was involved in the second iteration of the school. Though the name "Richardson" appears on the school's original crest,

Deryck feels confident that it was a reference to him rather than Jay.

Once more, Johnson found himself failing to answer the same question he had been asked dozens of times during the previous year's saga: Why not just stop? Was it ego or a warped sense of altruism? "50/50?" he guessed. "Every day it changes. Some days I was helping and some days it was pride. It goes back and forth."

For Deryck Richardson, who steered clear of the project after initial conversations, the issue was that Johnson learned the wrong lesson from his COF Academy days. "I think the first time, he truly had a bad hand dealt to him through the church. But the lesson he learned in that loss should have been, 'Get the money first before moving forward.' The lesson should not be, 'I can get this done without money.'"

In spite of his public confidence, behind the scenes, Andre was hitting the same barriers that Johnson had hit 12 months earlier. Once more, he had been in contact with "backers" who showed interest in helping finance the project. Once more, those people had pulled out without warning. Andre and others scrambled to use their own money to pay for housing, camps, travel, food, and other expenses. Along the way, the trail of unpaid debts that followed COF Academy continued under Bishop Sycamore's name.

"The idea was to try to be as self-sufficient as possible. But the truth of the matter is that's a hard model to follow, and I'm not a millionaire, so that's why we'd create other partnerships to bring in revenue to help the program," Andre told *Awful Announcing*, a well-known blog covering the business of sports media, in 2022. "So you have those partnerships you hope are going to materialize and be fruitful in helping you do what you're trying to do, and then people either lied or backed out.... When you're going into August and you're feeling good about the partnerships you have—and we really did—and then in September you start bringing in kids, and those [partnerships] aren't materializing. And now you have an issue, because I've got 40 kids here."

But even with dozens of kids under his responsibility, Peterson never took one major step: registering Bishop Sycamore as a school. For their first season, the head of the new program never submitted any documentation to the ODE to attempt to become certified as a high school, a step that even Johnson took. Legally speaking, there was no Bishop Sycamore High School in 2019—there was only the Bishop Sycamore football team.

Instead, Peterson attempted to create a partnership with an existing program, YouthBuild Columbus Community School. YouthBuild is a charter school that helps students earn high school diplomas or prepare for the General Educational

Development (GED) test. YouthBuild does not have an athletics program. In Peterson's mind, Bishop Sycamore would provide football playing opportunities to YouthBuild students and, in return, YouthBuild would provide an education. A YouthBuild employee even helped Peterson start the Bishop Sycamore Foundation, but would later say the foundation never got off the ground. Neither did the partnership.

Similar to the way COF Academy involved people within the AME Church but was disavowed by the larger body itself, Bishop Sycamore had recorded involvement with YouthBuild employees even after the relationship deteriorated. Husband and wife, Damond and Brandy Porter, both work at YouthBuild. Brandy is the business manager and also the individual who filed the paperwork to start the Bishop Sycamore Foundation in August of 2019. Brandy is experienced in starting a business, and has filed registrations in the state of Ohio for at least eight organizations in her lifetime. The businesses cover a broad scope, from a window tinting and detailing company to a daycare. Her filing for the Bishop Sycamore Foundation listed herself as the statutory agent, and also listed Damond and Peterson. In the details section describing the foundation, she described the organization as, "a foundation that provides education/sports to student athletes. We help youth/young adults that want to go off to college and have no solid support. Also children and young adults that struggle with education, we help give them the support that they need from us."

Damond is a teacher at YouthBuild and was also listed as a coach for Bishop Sycamore in 2019. And like a litany of others before and after, the pair found themselves embroiled in the Bishop Sycamore fallout. Damond was named in eviction lawsuits along with other members of the team in 2019 from the Griff Apartments in Columbus, along with Brandy's son, Maggness Fort Porter. Like others who became entangled with Bishop Sycamore, the Porters were no strangers to the courtroom. At least seven liens had been filed against the Porters in Franklin county between 2015 and 2018 due to unpaid debts.

The pair attempted to distance themselves from the school after the fallout in 2021, but their connection to the program would follow them. The Ohio Attorney General's office interviewed Brandy about her connection to the scheme, and she denied any involvement beyond helping to file the registration paperwork. When Brandy and Damond went to purchase a building in Columbus to use as a new home for their family in May of 2022, they received pushback from a zoning commission, citing their involvement with Bishop Sycamore. When the zoning commission asked if they could be trusted to make the improvements promised on the property given their past business involvement, the Porters claimed to have "no involvement" with Bishop Sycamore at all, saying that the school and the foundation were "two different entities." Despite the claim of no involvement, Damond did admit to a local Columbus journalist, DJ Byrnes, in an interview in his newsletter *The Rooster* that "he did coach for Bishop Sycamore, but claimed that he was unpaid, and quit after a month when he 'found out how bad it got.'" Brandy attempted to dissolve the Bishop Sycamore Foundation in April of 2022, but filed the wrong paperwork with the Ohio Secretary of State's office to do so. Dissolving the foundation would also incur a $50 fee. Brandy did not attempt to correct her paperwork, and the Bishop Sycamore Foundation is still an active nonprofit organization in Ohio.

Before their season, Bishop Sycamore ordered $6,000 worth of new uniforms and sent the bill to YouthBuild. The school canceled the partnership immediately, and sent a cease and desist letter to Peterson on August 31, 2019. In spite of that clear message, he continued to tout the relationship in order to schedule football games.

So with a new crop of teenagers involved in the second iteration of a program that was already showing signs of the same problems that had plagued COF Academy, Peterson and his team did what they knew how to do: they played football.

10

THE NUMBER ONE SCHEDULE IN THE WORLD

Although Bishop Sycamore's first year in existence was as tumultuous behind the scenes as it was in the COF Academy days, the debut season for the program's football team was much more in line with the trajectory of a reasonable program. Rather than scheduling an ambitious, eye-popping schedule, the 2019 Bishop Sycamore schedule featured teams that were closer to the new program's stature, like Indiana's Tri-State King's Crusaders or Pennsylvania's Kiski Prep. That first schedule also seemed designed to mitigate the heat on Peterson and Bishop Sycamore leadership that had been earned throughout Ohio as COF Academy.

Rather than scheduling a powerhouse in-state schedule that avoided travel, Bishop Sycamore would be embracing the rest of the country. In the 2019 season, they scheduled just one Ohio-based opponent, an October matchup against Cincinnati's Dohn Community High School, who went 2–7 that year. The ambitious scheduling of COF Academy had been replaced by a more reasonable approach, and it yielded the best results of either team. A 4–5 season was easily the most successful on-field performance of any Bishop Sycamore or COF Academy season. The team won two games—their season opener against Tri-State King's and a trip to Virginia's Catholic High School—in 66–6 and 48–0 blowouts, and lost another by a single score. It was a season that only the most ambitious schools would scoff at, and marked a brief turn toward a realistic approach to building a football program. But the season also introduced new flavors of chaos in the form of a cramped schedule and a free-flowing roster.

To alleviate the challenges of scheduling a season of high school football—especially as a team that didn't exist eight months earlier—Peterson and his team took a problem-solving attitude toward building their 2019 schedule. Rather than worrying about travel concerns, establishing a home field, or even when games would be played, Bishop Sycamore simply said, "Yes."

While most high school teams play on Friday nights with the occasional special game day sprinkled in, Bishop Sycamore took the opposite approach. Of their nine scheduled games, four fell on Saturday, four were on Friday, and another was played on a Thursday. And two of those games came back-to-back. After their 30–0 loss to Ensworth in Nashville, Tennessee, on Friday, October 11, the team made the four-hour drive to Dohn in Cincinnati to play a Saturday game less than 24 hours later. Against the odds, they won that second game 18–0. That kind of scheduling would become a recurring theme of the program, and one that Peterson and Roy Johnson never showed signs of worry about. "[Peterson] didn't really present it, he just said, 'You have a game today and play another game on Sunday,'" one player told *Awful Announcing* about a particularly demanding back-to-back. "And everyone was just confused and like, 'I guess.'" In one stretch, players played four games in 10 days.

A team full of exhausted players suffering through a demanding schedule with an unusually small roster seems to underline the importance of a quality trainer, but that wasn't an amenity offered by Bishop Sycamore. Even with many of them playing on both offense and defense in the same games, players said there was never a trainer around the team, and very little attention was paid to the well-being of the athletes who were powering the program. "Literally, if we got hurt, it was, 'We'll get you in the car and take you to the emergency room in the morning,'" one player told *Awful Announcing*. During the 2021 season, defensive lineman Jonah Sellers told the blog that he spent three games playing through an injury suffered on the second play of their season opener. In the fourth game of the season, he "fell out of nowhere" while running, and was treated on-site by a doctor employed by the facility. He would eventually be diagnosed with a torn ACL.

Whether as a response to barely having enough players to field a team, injured kids dropping by the game, or the demands of their unorthodox schedule, the Bishop Sycamore years saw administrators finding a solution in the quick churn and last-minute additions of players. While the New York recruiting of the COF Academy season was surprising to some, calling on out-of-state (and even out-of-the-country) players became a hallmark of the new program. Players were brought in from California, Michigan, Georgia, and beyond, and were introduced to the team with virtually no notice, preparation, or care. Sometimes, players would get to Ohio, join up with the team and start or play in the next game after a single practice—or less. Lineman Justin Daniel said at one point he met the team's starting center the day of the game. Sellers arrived in Columbus the day before his debut, dressing the next day with only a brief introduction to his teammates. "So we're playing the game, and we don't even practice, and I don't even know anyone on the team," Sellers said. "And [Johnson] was just like, 'Go with it,' and I was so confused. I'm like, 'I gotta get out of here.' It was so weird."

The new era of the program also stayed consistent with the COF Academy season in a variety of ways, including canceled games. Even the planned second game of the Bishop Sycamore football program would have to wait, as the team's matchup against Mainland High in Daytona Beach, Florida, was a last-minute cancellation. Somehow, with no history, Bishop Sycamore had been chosen to participate in the

Freedom Bowl, a Labor Day weekend kickoff tournament held in Georgia each year. In an interview with the *Daytona Beach News-Journal*, Freedom Bowl founder David Menard said he was swayed by the typical low-income players from single-parent households. He said he had spoken to "the Bishop Sycamore attorney," but did not name that person. "He acted more like a salesperson than an attorney, telling us about the program and what they were doing," Menard said.

Dylan Roye, the Freedom Bowl's director of operations, agreed with Menard's philanthropic approach to the scheduling. "We wanted to do something great for them. It's a brand new school. They were telling me that they were bringing in these less-privileged kids and giving them an opportunity to play football and get an education at a good institution. It came back to bite us in the butt."

Freedom Bowl officials were coy about why they canceled, but said it involved a "breach of contract" by Bishop Sycamore. They claimed to have upheld their own obligations, but apologized "for the massive inconvenience placed upon Daytona Mainland's coaches, players, faculty, and administration." Allegedly, Bishop Sycamore's staff failed to provide a roster ahead of an August 10 deadline set by the Freedom Bowl, and did not book hotel accommodations within the requested 30-day window after signing the contract. "When we contacted them about it, they said they would get it over.

They kept messing around a little bit," Roye said. "We just felt more comfortable not having Daytona Mainland come up and play against a team that we really didn't know much about."

Bishop Sycamore—or "the YouthBuild Centurions," as they were occasionally called due to their failed partnership with the Columbus school—helped ruin another home opener in their first season. Their scheduled game with West Virginia's Point Pleasant would have been the team's first home game of the season, but it was also canceled in September due to another alleged breach of contract on Bishop Sycamore's part. This time, the cancelation occurred because an opposing team finally took notice of the program's consistent use of players older than 18. Point Pleasant athletic director Kent Price told the *Point Pleasant Register* that "a series of contractual obligations" had not been met. He said Bishop Sycamore officials assured them that the program used only players that met National Federation of High Schools and West Virginia Secondary Sports Athletic Association guidelines, which require athletes to be 18 or younger. But Price said that when he got the team's roster, it showed "at least a handful" of players born in the year 2000 and others who had exhausted their high school eligibility. Price terminated the contract for the game. "They haven't met the obligations of the contract," he told the paper, noting that the roster issues would put his school in danger of liability issues. "In doing research, they have kids that are either fifth-year or 19-year-old kids on their roster and team. By our state rules, we cannot participate in a game that has fifth-year or 19-year-old kids on their roster and team. This is information that we didn't find out until this morning. I had a hard time getting the roster from the school, which finally showed up Monday morning. I called several times last week for the roster, but it didn't show up until today."

Within the context of their first 24 months of running a football program, and in spite of the multitude of issues, Johnson and Peterson could likely consider the first season of Bishop Sycamore a success. The team had flown under the radar, avoiding the scrutiny that COF Academy drew. They successfully scheduled and played nine games, and even managed to win four of them. It was a notable forward trajectory. But in the offseason between the 2019 and 2020 seasons, the COVID-19 pandemic hit, and that trajectory changed.

Overnight, it seemed that every high school football team's 2020 schedule was in disarray. Each element of scheduling football games became more challenging, from interstate travel and group activities like practices to conflicting state laws and cancellations due to outbreaks of the virus. So for the Bishop Sycamore staff, who never scheduled games far enough in advance, an opportunity presented itself. The team made it clear that they were willing to serve as replacements for games that needed to be moved. Suddenly, games were coming to them. And while a lengthy travel schedule had been a hallmark of the 2019 season, 2020 saw the team return to their Ohio roots.

They scheduled games against notable programs like St. Vincent–St. Mary, Massillon, St. Ignatius, Aurora, St. Edward, and Warren G. Harding in Ohio, before planning a Florida trip to end the season against Clearwater Academy and the biggest ticket matchup of all, IMG Academy. But once more, their early season plan had to be adjusted, as their planned opener against St. Vincent–St. Mary was canceled after their athletic director was warned about Bishop Sycamore's past. The game against Clearwater would follow. St. Ignatius' program from their 2020 game against Bishop Sycamore showed that they knew exactly who they were playing. The program says, "Bishop Sycamore is a non-OHSAA school" and mentions that Donovan McClendon would be playing in the game as a "fifth-year senior." The program also included some statistics from Bishop Sycamore's game the week prior against Massillon, which let the fans know it should be an easy win. "J'Quan Billups-Clark, Joshua Logan, Tay Lowe, and Jacolby Jackson all saw multiple carries. As a team, the Centurions netted –26 rushing yards." Another section, simply labeled "miscues," noted that Bishop Sycamore "had two high snaps on punts go for safeties and 18 penalties for 108 yards. They'll look to clean those up on Saturday."

Throughout the course of the season, Bishop Sycamore picked up one commonality with other schools: they didn't have in-person classes. After the failed YouthBuild partnership attempt, Johnson and Peterson took a new approach in 2020, attempting to register with the Ohio Department of Education and trying two more educational partnerships. In July of 2020, they sent a document to the ODE that described Bishop Sycamore as "an innovative academically accredited school Partnering with Advancing Sciences Worldwide and Innovation Science and Education."

"With ISE innovative education platform and ASW," the letter reads, "the Bishop Sycamore partnership makes this High School one of the best academic institutions in the country." But that partnership would never get off the ground. The president of ASW told 10TV in 2022 that the organization "never had any partnership with a school called Bishop Sycamore and we never provided them any educational materials."

Next, they tried a partnership with Graduation Alliance, a Utah-based organization that offers "dropout recovery programs and alternative education academies" as well as online courses. The partnership began in October 2020, which meant that Bishop Sycamore had no formal classroom element to its program for more than a year between 2019 and 2020. The agreement with Graduation Alliance would last only five months.

But to Johnson, this dynamic made his approach completely reasonable. "Everyone" was taking online classes, so what was wrong with his plan? "People say, 'Bishop Sycamore's not a school.' Why's it not a school? 'It's not a school because, at the address you had, kids weren't attending classes.' Well, they weren't, were they? Well, why weren't they attending classes? Because nobody was. It was COVID. Nobody was going to school," he said with a huge laugh. But two years later, Peterson would admit that, during this time, class was barely a part of Bishop Sycamore.

"Here's the thing about education: For anybody who needed it or wanted it, it was there," he told *Awful Announcing*. "But there could have been more control. What we needed that we didn't have was our own space, because if we have our own space, I can control it, like, 'Okay, everybody get up, and we're going to be in the classroom from eight to two, and we're going to do this together.'... And when you don't have your own space, your own facilities, it gets harder. Because I can't go in there and see what you're doing."

In the months that would follow, players had differing opinions about how much schooling Bishop Sycamore provided and whether students ever participated in that process.

One anonymous player said he took his classwork seriously, while Daniel said he used his computer to play video games. "Online schooling can work," the anonymous player said. "But you're going to have to buy computers for all of the kids. You're going to need a place where they can all go [and study]."

Receiver Devante Jackson doesn't like it when people call Bishop Sycamore a "fake school," but admits that he never saw anyone taking classes during his time with the team. "We signed up for school, we just never *did* school. We were just waiting for that time, 'Alright, it's time to go to class.' But we never got that call. We never got that text, 'Alright, we're about to start school.'... In the time I was there, we didn't do schoolwork, but we had signed up for our classes."

One player told *Complex*, anonymously, that players "didn't start school until months after enrolling in August" in spite of a "brochure" that said classes would be through Franklin University in Columbus.

Franklin University spokesperson Sherry Mercurio told the *Columbus Dispatch* that a partnership with Bishop Sycamore never came to fruition. "Representatives from Bishop Sycamore did reach out to us in 2020 to discuss the opportunity to lease space. However, no contract was ever signed," she said, "Representatives from Franklin University have reached out to Bishop Sycamore on multiple occasions to request that our address be removed from their website since there is no relationship between the two institutions."

But none of these stories faze Johnson. For him, these players didn't deserve an education they weren't willing to work hard for, and it wasn't his responsibility to force them. They had arrived at Bishop Sycamore because their football or academic careers didn't go as planned, and he gave them a chance. To him, it was black and white. He pointed to one player who made a YouTube video claiming he never went to class, and said he spoke to another player that made fun of the video. "One of the other players laughed and was like, 'Bro, you never showed up,'" Johnson said. "You got a free laptop that you were supposed to use to go to school, and you stole it and sold it. Then, you went into the apartment that had TVs and you stole the TVs off the wall and sold them. You beat up a kid on the team who was 16 when you were 18. You did so many things wrong, but you're telling people there was no school. You never went to school! You graduated already!" Whether players made an effort or not was ultimately irrelevant. Graduation Alliance told the ODE that their relationship with Bishop Sycamore fizzled by January 2021. It was the last documented attempt at establishing an educational component at Bishop Sycamore.

With another year of tumult came more disappointing results on the field. Bishop Sycamore went without a win in 2020, posting an 0–6 record that included losses of 35–0, 33–6, 31–8, 35–8, 37–14, and 56–6 in their biggest game of the season, a matchup against powerhouse IMG Academy.

* * *

Although the football team monopolized Johnson's focus, he was also dealing with more of his own personal legal issues than ever. On March 7, 2020, Johnson was arrested for domestic violence, assault, and disorderly conduct. According to a police report from the Delaware County Sheriff's Office, Johnson's ex-girlfriend called the police after Johnson threatened to take her car. "He kept insisting on taking my car keys. He said he would take them if I don't give them. I kept insisting he get a ride and leave," she says in the report, "He grabbed all his belongings and said, 'I'm taking the car, period.' I forewarned I would call the cops and he said, 'Try, go ahead, see where it gets you.' He said they can't make him leave. He purposely got his bank card sent here today so it looks like he gets mail here. I've been asking him to leave and he refuses. I kept trying to grab my keys out of his hoodie pocket, and he said, 'Don't touch me.' I never touched him. I was trying to get the keys without ever touching him. He threw me up against the wall and said once again he will take the keys no matter what and not to touch him. His phone fell out of his pocket so I grabbed it and said I would give him the phone back when he gives me my keys. He pushed me into the couch, put his one knee with his weight into my back, busted my lip, and I kept ahold of his phone til he finally grabbed it from me. He took my keys and threw them outside in the dark. I ran outside to try and look for them, ran to the neighbors' house, hid behind a tree, and called 911."

Responding officers described Johnson's ex-girlfriend as "crying and fearful with minor cuts to her face," but said Johnson was "calm."

"I arrived on the scene and met with the caller," said Deputy Jonathan Hicks, the arresting officer. "I immediately observed [the victim] had a bloody lip. It was observed on the bottom, left side of her face. She explained that she got into an altercation with her boyfriend, Leroy Johnson. She stated that he took her car keys and when she attempted to get them back, he then hit her in the lip … Leroy stated he never got into a physical altercation with [her.] He denied ever touching her. He stated he never took her keys and they were inside the kitchen drawer the entire time. Leroy was placed under arrest based on the statement by [the victim] and the visible physical injury. Leroy did not have any physical injuries to his person."

Johnson claims he's "very reluctant" to talk about the incident because he doesn't want to give the impression that he's "not being accountable for what I did or that I think it's okay to have a domestic violence situation going on." But that didn't stop him from downplaying what happened. "There are certain things that are really hard to talk about," he said. "I feel like if it was anywhere else, I wouldn't have gotten arrested. But because it's Delaware and a little White girl, I got arrested. You can get the records and the video link of when they arrested me. I'll never forget the attorney said, 'You look shocked.' Of course I was shocked! There was no violence!"

Johnson is adamant that he didn't hit her. He claims his friends were outside and he was simply trying to leave. He scoffed at the idea that violence from him would have resulted in a bloody lip. Johnson comes from a family with a father who boxed. So if he had hit her, he claimed, it would have been worse. "I was like, 'If I had punched her, she'd still be in the air right now,'" he said with a laugh. "So then we go to court and everything got dropped, but I have to take an anger management course. But that's just my opinion about it. She might tell you something different."

Who was this woman to Johnson? "She's just some chick I was dating," he said, before admitting they were still together.

That's a good thing, right?

"I guess," he deadpanned.

Johnson spent three days in jail before posting bond. He pled not guilty to the charges, and the victim received a protection order ensuring Johnson had to stay away from her and her residence. He was required to wear a GPS electronic ankle monitor. However, Johnson didn't follow the requirements. On June 1, 2020, his bond was revoked and a new warrant was issued for his arrest. In a court hearing on June 5, his lawyer was able to get the warrant set aside with promises that Johnson would follow his requirements. On August 4, he received a deal, pleading guilty to criminal mischief in exchange for the other charges being dismissed. His GPS ankle monitor was removed and he was given one year of probation and a suspended 60-day jail sentence. He also received a fine and had to pay court costs, totaling $1,267.20, that were to be paid by November 10. After the hearing, Johnson did what he does best: he disappeared.

Johnson did not pay the fine by the deadline and he did not appear at any of the Delaware County Court hearings set up to determine his punishment for not following the court's orders. On June 30, 2021, after multiple failed attempts to get ahold of Johnson, his non-payment was officially deemed a violation of his probation and a warrant was issued for his arrest. In all three games of Bishop Sycamore's 2021 season, Johnson was a wanted man. It wasn't until Bishop Sycamore's season fell apart and Johnson found himself in the limelight that he turned himself in. On September 8, 2021, he pled guilty to the probation violations. As punishment, his probation was extended until March 5, 2022, and he was still required to pay the fine. Two days later, Johnson asked the court to officially terminate his probation. But there was an outstanding issue—Johnson hadn't paid his fine. The motion to terminate his probation was granted, but a private collection agency was hired to track down the fine. It still hasn't been paid.

The incident didn't close the chapter between Johnson and this woman, however. On February 21, 2022, Johnson was charged with aggravated menacing for making threats over the phone and through text messages to her. The next day, a warrant was issued for his arrest. It wasn't until April 6, 2022, that Johnson appeared before the court through an attorney. He pled not guilty to the charges, and asked for the warrant to be set aside. Delaware County was not making the same mistake twice, and denied his motion. Three weeks later, Johnson was arrested and bonded out the same day. Like his last charge, Johnson decided to take a deal, pleading guilty to a lesser charge of menacing, a fourth-degree misdemeanor that represents a significantly smaller charge than aggravated menacing, a first-degree misdemeanor. Johnson was given a suspended 30-day jail sentence, a year of probation, and was required to pay court costs and a fine. This time, he owed

$712. He has never paid. A court hearing was scheduled for November 15, 2022, for Johnson to appear and explain why he has not paid his fine. He did not attend.

Johnson's run-ins with the law persist. On December 5, 2022, charges were filed against Johnson in Franklin County for shoplifting from a Best Buy in Grove City, Ohio, a suburb of Columbus. A police report of the incident says that Johnson went into the store and bought a variety of items on store credit using an alias—Tristan Hershtol. After fraudulently purchasing the items, Johnson stole a Blink Video Doorbell on his way out of the store, which was what prompted his arrest. Johnson pled not guilty, with the trial yet to take place.

* * *

Amid a winless season, Johnson had plenty to worry about within his own team as well. First came the parents, who frustrated Johnson by questioning the school and its leaders' methods.

But Johnson said he set a precedent that those parents could complain to him—rather than someone like Peterson—even if he managed to find a way to consider those complaints unjust. "Parents wouldn't dare question the coaching staff of IMG. IMG or whoever are going to set a standard that's a little different than the standard I want to set because we were a different situation," he said. "I'm not an idiot. If you have a traditionally winning program that never loses and parents complain, you can easily just turn around and say, 'You can go somewhere else.' I didn't have that luxury because we weren't a traditional program."

And while Johnson deftly avoided his own legal consequences, Bishop Sycamore's strategy of recruiting players with checkered pasts began to wear on Johnson. He said he knew of two of his former players that were killed after they left the program—a frightening ratio for a team as short-lived as Bishop Sycamore and COF Academy. Johnson said he doesn't know if those players' deaths are at all related to him or the program, or if his association with them was simply a result of his recruiting strategy. But ultimately, he doesn't take responsibility.

"One player—a kid who kept getting kicked off the team and stole money—went on YouTube and said, 'Because Roy was afraid to come pick him up in the hood, he got left there and got killed,'" Johnson said. "Now, if you talk to the guys on the team, they'd tell you they don't think Roy is afraid of bad neighborhoods because Detroit, Cincinnati, Chicago are way worse than Columbus, Ohio. So I'm not sure why I would have been afraid to pick him up. What they won't tell you is that they broke into a car, stole money from a tutor, beat up a kid on the team, were always high and smoking weed, their probation officers couldn't find them. There were so many things that went into that situation. So how do I respond to that? What do I say? Do I air out the business of a dead kid?"

To other players, including one anonymous interview with *Complex*, recruiting those players was a danger in and of itself. "We took a dude on the team that was straight out of jail and put him on the team when he graduated in 2019," one player said. "Straight out of the cell. We couldn't fly on the plane to IMG Academy because people had warrants for their arrest." But, as always, Johnson sees his efforts as philanthropic. To him, those players were already on a bad path. He just tried to help.

"They have so many different backgrounds and so many things going on. I'm trying to help them but I can only do so much.... But then, after I help you guys, if it didn't turn out the way that you felt it should have turned out, I turn into your number one enemy."

For players with less tragic stories, time at Bishop Sycamore earned mixed reviews. Devante Jackson joined the program in the 2021 season as a graduate of Lorraine High School after missing his senior year due to COVID-19. He had received an offer to go to Ohio Dominican University on a partial scholarship, but he didn't have the upfront money needed to allow him to commit. So when a friend told him about Bishop Sycamore and he saw the schedule, he jumped at the opportunity. And when he arrived in Columbus and got situated in his new living arrangements, a shared apartment among a few players, he found it "nice" and felt that some players simply "couldn't adjust" to the situation. "Some people couldn't live in that type of environment. Say you had two people in your room, some people come into that environment … and couldn't adapt to it. It definitely depends on the person. Some people, where they came from, probably had it better and they weren't used to it. But a lot of the people on the team, that's just how they grew up. So it wasn't really a problem.

"You play the number one schedule in the world, you don't care how you live."

Some players, however, cared how they lived. And because Johnson and Peterson were still exaggerating the living, playing, and educating aspects of Bishop Sycamore, players felt betrayed. In an interview with *Complex*, one anonymous player called Johnson "a liar," "a thief," and "probably worse things." But he said the worst thing Johnson did was to sell "false dreams" to his players. "Like telling your players you're gonna have X, Y, Z, we're gonna fund this and that, and not having any of that provided for your kids. I don't know what program the schooling is with, but not making sure your kids are getting the proper education. It's cool to check in every once in a while to see how your kids are in school. We didn't even start till three months after the fact. So I'd say school, selling false dreams, and funding. I think that's the concept of lying, selling false dreams."

But was Johnson "selling" anything? Like many others related to Bishop Sycamore, the answer to that question varies greatly depending on who you ask. Johnson himself, for example, claims no one ever paid tuition, a point he reiterates repeatedly as a defense for the living conditions and general lack of organization at the program. "It probably should've been an IMG situation, where you go into a banquet hall every day and all the food is brought out. But you didn't have that shit in high school. Now, you come here and complain about the food. Guess what? Your mom didn't pay any tuition. If you wanted to do better, guess what your parents could have done? Sent you money. It was free." The only time Johnson admits to taking any money from kids was on a camp tour during the summer of 2020, where the team charged players $1,500 to participate in a tour that went all the way from Youngstown State to the University of Houston and back, staying in hotels along the way and participating in a variety of football camps. "It's not like we charged them for tuition," he specified. "They called it tuition or whatever they called it. Whatever the paperwork said. But trust me, it wasn't tuition."

But Andre Peterson has a different take. He told a reporter with *League of Justice* that he switched to charging tuition in 2021 so that he could pay for apartments for the players. Peterson said he and Johnson spent tuition money on housing, food, and other amenities. "With any business you try to make things work out the best way possible, and so sometimes those things don't always work out the way that you want them to, so you try to correct them or you try to get help in doing it. You try to make sure that whatever you're lacking, that you have. It wasn't just 'Well, we didn't have a place.' We were securing places that we couldn't use or weren't open just because of COVID, period. And so it wasn't because we didn't have a place. I can understand the people's perception of that part of it, but that's a growing pain for any business."

Peterson told *USA Today* in a separate interview that tuition was $2,000. In the same quote, however, he said that the program had 75 or 80 students, a number their team never approached. Jackson said he was charged a $1,000 "deposit," but knew that other players—especially those who didn't have the money—didn't have to pay.

By 2021, Johnson had gotten even more brazen—or desperate, depending on who you ask—in his lying attempts. Bishop Sycamore racked up more lawsuits for failing to pay, including bus transportation, passing invalid checks to pay for a hotel, and a variety of other unpaid debts. In one instance,

Ray Holtzclaw, whose son, Judah, briefly played quarterback at Bishop Sycamore, claims Johnson stuck him with a bill for hotel rooms worth thousands of dollars. He claimed he would pay back Holtzclaw, who told *Awful Announcing* he never saw a dime. "One thing with being a parent and coach and just somebody trying to help these boys out, is a lot of these kids didn't have much," Holtzclaw said. "For them to get that extra chance to play football is important, but they watch everything. They see everything. They hear you saying one thing, and then when they see you do another, like not paying your bills ... that paints a different picture. You can't do that."

But in spite of every speed bump along the way—the angry parents, the legal issues, the unpaid debts, the lack of education, and a flailing football program—2021 was set to be Bishop Sycamore's most ambitious season yet. The days of a reasonable, winnable schedule were gone, replaced by yet another extreme slate of games that landed Bishop Sycamore in the number four position of MaxPreps top ten schedules in all of high school football for 2021. Games once again included a variety of powerhouses, including Ohio powers Archbishop Hoban and St. Edward, as well as the return of the biggest name of them all: IMG Academy.

In the spring of 2021, Johnson even tried to recruit his first relative celebrity coach, reaching out to former Ohio State and NFL quarterback Cardale Jones. "Let me tell y'all something right now. I kid y'all not, I'll show y'all the text messages. Bishop Sycamore, Roy Johnson offered me $85,000 in April to be the offensive coordinator," Jones told *Lettermen Row*. "He already told me he locked down a big-time game versus IMG on ESPN here in Columbus." Jones claimed he didn't accept the offer because he was still trying to find an NFL or professional football career, but felt that the offer was a real one.

During this period, Johnson even tried to add an international flair to the program. The team started recruiting players from overseas, and Johnson bragged in an interview with the *High School Football America* podcast that he was trying to add players from London, Croatia, and elsewhere in Europe. One of those players was Kofi Taylor-Barrocks, an English recruit who was a hot international prospect in the class of 2022. The linebacker was part of the NFL Academy in London, a program aimed at developing European talent. Taylor-Barrocks turned down the offer from Bishop Sycamore, which was an easy decision, as he ended up signing with Colorado after receiving 10 scholarship offers. Johnson also attempted to lure Canadian brothers Matthew and Mark Armah to Columbus, but failed there as well. In spite of that, all three players appeared on a 2021 Bishop Sycamore roster. None of them ever moved to Columbus, agreed to join the program, or played for the team.

Johnson, Peterson, and the 2021 program were struggling to find players, but had assembled a schedule that was tougher than ever. So to supplement the program's roster, Johnson got desperate and returned to the same scattershot recruiting style that had defined the early days of the COF Academy program. In an attempt to try and flesh out the roster, he used a technique reminiscent of high schoolers who are desperate for dates—he began taking wild shots on social media and approaching players through direct messages, racking up an outrageous number of attempted contacts in a short period of time. From May 29 through August 24, 2021, the official Bishop Sycamore Twitter account tweeted some variation of "dm us" or "dm me" at 288 different students. The football players they were targeting were based all over the country, but shared one important commonality: they had all already graduated high school. For a team getting ready to participate in a "national high school showcase," Bishop Sycamore wasn't concerned with building a roster of actual high schoolers. That frantic recruiting push was largely unproductive.

As expected, the season got off to an inauspicious start with a dominant 38–0 win by Hoban (in another classic Bishop Sycamore Thursday night matchup). Along the way, even players on opposing teams knew that something was amiss with the mystery program they faced. "We were looking for a game Week 1 and we get assigned this prep team, and we're like, 'We're going to get whooped,'" said Hoban lineman Bryce Sisak. And by the time his team was leading by double digits and the reality of the situation had set in, he said he and his teammates actually started worrying about the safety of their teammates playing against an opponent who was drastically less talented, but physically intimidating enough to do damage. "I think we played starters like 20 or 30 snaps [before backups came in.] I think there was some danger, size-wise and in experience. Those offensive lineman, I've gone against big offensive lineman, it's not new to me, but like a freshman or a sophomore going up against a guy who's like 6'8" and 330, it's a different experience." Sisak said, "there's a gap that's there that needs to be bridged." Sisak didn't mind the game, though, and found it memorable. "I think it was a unique experience. I'm definitely not going to experience anything like that again."

After the Hoban game, on August 22, the Bishop Sycamore program hit a new low: asking for money. The program was struggling so much that one of the players, Khalil Davis, started a GoFundMe to try to raise money for the team under his own name. Davis' name does not appear on any of the Bishop Sycamore 2021 rosters, though he did provide a photo of himself with the team as verification for the fundraiser. The GoFundMe set a goal of $20,000, and reads:

> "We are Bishop Sycamore a new football program getting established in Columbus, Ohio. We play a national scheduled

> which is ranked 4th in the nation. We have gather young men from all over the country in the pursuit of a similar goal. We currently need your assistant with helping these young men achieve their goals and inspire other young men to do the same. It takes a community to raise a child please be that community and help these young men! Please help us with funding team meals, travel expenses, and equipment cost. Check us out on Instagram and twitter: @_Bishopfootball."

The account raised $140 before being shut down.

A week later, Bishop Sycamore traveled to Pennsylvania program Sto-Rox, where they lost a 19–7 game. But after that loss, they didn't have a week to recover; they had two days. In a signature Bishop Sycamore move, their big IMG Academy matchup was to be played the Sunday after the Friday matchup. To compensate, Johnson flew in two recruits from London in between the Sto-Rox loss and the Sunday game. Both stepped onto the field against IMG with no prior introduction or training.

But by that point in 2021, Johnson had no idea that the marquee matchup of which he had dreamed for years wouldn't be his national coming-out party, but would instead mark the downfall of Bishop Sycamore on national television.

11

TRENDING ON TWITTER

The morning of August 29, 2021, felt different to Roy Johnson. In general, he considered himself—like many coaches—a person who tried to treat every game day the same. He had a morning pregame routine, tried not to let himself feel too high or too low, and didn't do much bragging before the game. But today, the team he was coaching was playing the nation's biggest high school football team, and they were doing it in front of a national television audience on ESPN. And far before the cameras were rolling, even the monotonous details of the day were a new sensation for him.

"It definitely feels different because it's the NFL Hall of Fame field," he said. "I think the rest of the team—I say I think because I didn't ask them—felt like it was an honor to play there. I don't think anyone would deny that. Of course it's a big deal. When you get to the game, it's the same thing. You have to go get the headsets up in the box upstairs and it's like a maze in that place. It was difficult getting that together and making sure the headsets worked and all of that."

Between those first moments in the stadium and kickoff, things get fuzzy for Johnson. Frantically running around to set up headsets, put players through warmups, and preparing for the game, he didn't have time to think about what was happening.

"You get so tied up in making sure everyone is eating breakfast and getting on the bus and has their equipment, nobody forgot everything, everyone is awake," he said. "I spent more time focusing on that. It's like there's so much that goes into it, you don't really get to enjoy the moment at that point. That part I don't really remember. It's kind of like a wedding. You have everything planned and you're ready for this big day, but most of the time you're like, 'I've gotta make sure uncle so-and-so shows up on time; I've gotta make sure Mom and Dad get picked up; I've gotta make sure of this and that.' And then during the ceremony you're so nervous you don't get a chance to reflect and enjoy it until it's over."

But in front of his team, Johnson tried to put on a calm face. The Bishop Sycamore squad had never been the most punctual, responsible bunch, so he wanted to at least try to help them treat the day like any of their other games. "It was a normal day, but it was ESPN. I wanted to make sure that everyone was there and had their uniforms and were together and nobody left anything at the hotel. It was more like taking a parent or leadership role than anything else. I knew we were going to be on TV. And not just regular TV—*TV-TV*. You double and triple check everything.

Everyone here? Not missing anybody? None of you idiots fell asleep in the room?"

In the moments before kickoff, Johnson did take a moment to breathe. He had been calling friends and family to let them know that the big day had arrived—his team was going to play on national TV. Before he put his phone away, he checked back in to remind people to tune in. But just a couple hours later, he wished he hadn't.

The IMG game wasn't just big for Johnson, it was, for many Bishop Sycamore players, the payoff for coming to the school in the first place. For Devante Jackson, a matchup against IMG Academy and the chance to play at the Pro Football Hall of Fame had been the very first selling point for the program. The summer before signing on with Bishop Sycamore, he was talking to a friend who was planning on joining the team. "He was basically telling me, 'It's this school where all the top people around the world are going to be playing there, and we play IMG,' and that was one of the main things, honestly. That's the biggest high school in the world." He remembers that friend being elated "because we play IMG at the Canton Hall of Fame."

"When I heard that, I'm like, 'Dang, the Canton Hall of Fame? Playing against IMG on national TV on ESPN? You can't really beat that.... That's your chance, trying to be different."

The team stayed in a hotel close to the stadium and got their equipment for the game just the day before. "The next thing you know, we're at the Hall of Fame," Jackson recalled. But quickly, the mood among the team started to shift. Players walked on the field and receivers ran routes to get used to the turf. Back in the locker room, players were arguing because of a perceived clash of mindsets. "Some people weren't straightening up. They were acting too happy, not serious; they weren't focused."

Moments after kickoff, it was clear that the team wasn't ready. Almost immediately, Jackson, who was injured and couldn't play, could tell that it was going to be a long day. "IMG came up with a good start and a good kickoff return and then it was like the fourth play of the game and they scored on us. Everybody just lost hope. We went on offense and got broken down and it was just all bad from there. It was like everybody was so shocked we were playing IMG it felt like everyone was in a state [tournament] game that they had never been to."

Johnson admits that even then, he "subconsciously" knew they couldn't beat IMG Academy. They were there to get on a big stage and get tape. But he quickly began to worry about "keeping them in control" because the kids were getting emotional. "They were upset. Some were [struggling] more than others. Then the Turk happens."

"The Turk" is something Johnson says he invented himself. He says some people call it quicksand. It's a term almost any coach, leader, or even parent has seen before. The Turk is more of a feeling than anything, and once it begins, it's difficult to reverse.

"Things start going wrong, and when things start going wrong it spreads. We're losing, the score is bad, the weather gets bad, two of the kids switch jerseys and the mother is mad because they're announcing another kid's name and not her kid's name. Now parents are getting upset and they're coming down. You've got players on the sideline saying, 'If you had put me in, this game wouldn't have gotten out of control.' The Turk sets in. Quicksand."

At the end of the first quarter, IMG had a 23–0 lead that felt generous to Bishop Sycamore. Players looked physically and mentally outmatched, and the game had the feel of a professional team playing an amateur group of players. With the score at 30–0 midway through the second quarter, ESPN commentators Anish Shroff and Tom Luginbill started to level with the audience.

"Bishop Sycamore told us they had a number of Division I prospects on their roster," Shroff said. "To be frank, a lot of that, we could not verify. They did not show up in our database; they did not show up in the database of other recruiting services. So okay, if that's what you're telling us, fine, that's how we'll take it in. But from what we've seen so far, this is not a fair fight. There's got to be a point where you do worry about health and safety."

"I already am worried about it," Luginbill replied, clearly frustrated. "This could potentially be dangerous, given the circumstances and the mismatch we have here. Quite honestly, Bishop Sycamore doesn't have not only the front-line players, but they don't have the depth in case something were to happen to that roster with maybe a kid or two [injured] here in the remaining two and a half quarters here."

In the days that followed the game, ESPN would immediately point their finger at Paragon Marketing, a sports and entertainment brand and promoter with a history of setting up high school sports to air on the network. "We regret that this happened and have discussed it with Paragon, which secured the matchup and handles the majority of our high school event scheduling," an ESPN statement read. "They have ensured us that they will take steps to prevent this kind of situation from happening moving forward."

But the scheduling of the matchup didn't just happen thanks to Paragon, it started with Joe Maimone, the vice president of sales at music industry giant Billboard. Away from his job with Billboard, Maimone runs Prep Gridiron Logistics, a high school football–focused organization that describes itself as "Your stress-free resource for quality, interstate scheduling." The company curates an online scheduling database for high schools looking for games and attempting to put together quality matchups. But for Maimone, not all schools are created equal. As he told *The Athletic*, Maimone has "pet projects" that he tries to provide extra exposure for thanks to missions that he sees as worthy. One of those pet projects was Bishop Sycamore. When asked how the lowly Bishop Sycamore, whose previous season records were available for anyone to see, managed to wind up on IMG Academy's schedule, he repeated the usual refrain: there was simply no one else. "The blueblood Ohio programs, like St. Ed's and St. Ignatius, none of them stepped up to play this game," he told *The Athletic*. "You can't blame Bishop Sycamore for doing that. They're the only ones who had the courage to do so. They should be rewarded, not freaking lambasted."

Between Maimone's Prep Gridiron and Paragon, the organizations had finally found an opponent for IMG Academy, and the game was set to broadcast as part of the GEICO ESPN High School Football Kickoff, an annual showcase of talented teams in the weeks leading up to NCAA football and NFL kickoff weekends. The matchup served as the weekend's finale, the seventh game of the weekend with a 1:30 PM kickoff time on Sunday afternoon and one of just two matchups that aired on the main ESPN channel.

No matter how much responsibility lies at the feet of Maimone and Prep Gridiron, Paragon president Rashid Ghazi was already publicly apologizing the very next day. "The vetting process and the issues with the matchup are 100 percent on Paragon," he told *The Athletic*. "As the guy who founded the ESPN relationship and the president of the company, it's really 100 percent on me."

As Shroff and Luginbill made their feelings known, the internet was becoming aware of what was happening on ESPN. On Twitter, Ohio high school football beat reporters began wondering aloud who Bishop Sycamore was. Before the game reached halftime, Akron reporter Ryan Isley posted, "Imagine that. Bishop Sycamore didn't give the TV guys an accurate or complete roster. This is the 'roster' we were given when they played Archbishop Hoban last week ..." and included a photo of a 26-person roster broken down by positions like "O/D Line" and "Athletes."

Tweets like those caught the eye of Ben Koo, owner and editor of *Awful Announcing*. Koo, coincidentally a Columbus resident, had seen the press release for the event and wondered why he had never heard of this school playing IMG. And at first, he assumed he was simply watching the story of ESPN making a bad match. "I'm like, 'What's this about?' I thought there was an 'ESPN got duped' story here because this team just wasn't good. And then more and more people are tweeting about them and who they were." In the moment, he reached out to ESPN public relations, who passed him along to Ghazi, who told him that he "also felt a little duped." But Koo felt Ghazi's tone didn't match the urgency of the situation. Koo remembers thinking, "He's just not grasping how viral this is getting."

In Akron, just down the road from Canton, Bryce Sisak and his teammates had watched the game involving the team they beat 38–0 just 10 days earlier. He admitted it was a fun watch. "The thing that struck me the most was that they were playing IMG. Like, we had just handed them their lunch, and these dudes are going to go play IMG's national team? They're going to get hurt. It was pretty entertaining to watch, and the announcers were trying to debunk what was happening. It was pretty entertaining to keep up with it. All these articles kept popping up and all the kids on my team are like, 'There's no way we just played a fake school.' So we did our own research and [we're] like, 'This kid has fake offers!' It was so bizarre."

It didn't take long for news of the game to reach Ulysses Hall. After years away from the program, he said he was shocked to see the name Bishop Sycamore on TV, shocked to see the name of the head coach, and shocked at the claims about their roster. "They were like, 'Coach Roy.' First of all, I'm like, 'Why is Roy coaching?' Two, I was like,

'Wow, they're on ESPN. How in the hell?' I'm like, 'Okay, maybe they've really got funding.' Then I'm listening and watching the game and they're mentioning they had all these DI players and all of that. I'm looking at this roster and I don't know any of these guys. I'm a recruiter. I literally follow what's going on. I'm looking at the names, and I don't know any of these guys. I'm like, 'You're lying to ESPN.'"

The game ended in a 58–0 win for IMG Academy that included a variety of plays that were hilarious to some and cringeworthy to others, highlighted by an attempted punt by quarterback Trillian Harris that was blocked and returned for a touchdown. Back in the Bishop Sycamore locker room, the fairytale was over. Johnson's phone was bombarded by more than 100 texts and notifications, and it wasn't good news. "By the time you get a chance to sit down and think, 'I can't believe after these long years that we finally made it to such a big stage and be on television,' to then get phone calls after phone calls after phone calls of just stuff that has nothing to do with something that should have been a great day, it was actually quite disappointing. My close friends are like, 'As long as you've been doing this and all the guys we know, why is a guy on ESPN talking about you guys so badly?' I was like 'What do you mean?' That part was hard."

He even had a text from Maimone, who Johnson said reached out to tell him, "The announcers on ESPN are making you look like a fool." The first call Johnson made was to an old friend—who he declined to name because of a "colorful background." Johnson and that friend have an old inside joke where they label problems on a scale of six hours to six months. When he asked his friend which version of a problem he was facing, the friend already knew it would be serious. This was a six-month problem.

The players felt it, too. Jackson said everyone looked at their phones in the aftermath of the game, and players experienced a similar flood of notifications. "There were a lot of Twitter updates, a lot of trolling going on, a lot of DMs on Instagram. There was one point in time where I had to turn off my notifications. That's just how it was. It felt like we were in the NFL, how many people were DMing us. We were trending on Twitter for like two weeks straight." Some moments, it felt like something cool to be part of. Other times, when strangers on the internet were harassing and insulting the players, it was less fun. "Why would you do something like that? What if someone was saying something like that to your mom or your dad or your grandma or someone?"

While the players rode home together on the bus, Johnson went home separately, spending the car ride home quieter than usual. However, he doesn't regret not being on the bus.

"They're grown men," Johnson said about the group of individuals he'd just put on the field in a high school showcase meant for children. "There was nothing I could do." The game had been a blow, but Johnson was already trying to make sense of how to move on.

Twenty-four hours later, he was no longer the coach.

Andre Peterson, now acting as the director of Bishop Sycamore, went on a press tour to do damage control, telling *USA Today* that he fired Johnson and reassuring the outlet that the organization he was running was a real school.

"There's nothing that I've gotten out of this that would constitute it as a scam because I'm not gaining anything financially from what we're doing," he told *USA Today*. "The reality of it is that I have a son that's also in the program and has been in the program for four years."

The same day, he told Columbus TV news station WBNS–10TV that Johnson and Bishop Sycamore had mutually parted ways. In that interview, he revealed that they had been paid by Paragon to play in the game, but declined to say how much, citing a non-disclosure agreement. He would only admit that it was enough to cover travel expenses, and continued to defend the project. "The main focus of the school has always been to help young men and, whether it was grades or anything like that, to help them get into school. It's just—it's just honestly been a shock." Peterson told *USA Today* that it had been suggested to him that Bishop Sycamore shut down. "I can't," he said. "I have kids that are dependent on what we do. For me to start all over and send them home and say 'Hey, you work it out for yourself,' would be a disservice to them. I just know that we have things to get right. We have to make this to where every question that's asked, there's an answer to it."

Later, Peterson would admit to *Awful Announcing* that Bishop Sycamore was never paid the $1,000 they expected for the game. They did, however, make an effort to find another money-making avenue through their most public moment. In an attempt to capitalize off of their new fame, or infamy, they began selling merchandise. On August 31, just two days after the game, the threadbare website at BishopSycamore.org was scrubbed. The "online school" no longer had an online presence. Now, in its place, the team was promoting a spirit store, where you could buy Bishop Sycamore branded t-shirts, hoodies, sweatpants, and polos. It's unknown how much money, if any, they made from selling merchandise, but the website is still actively selling the items.

Through that period, Johnson stopped doing interviews. In the hours and days after his face first appeared on ESPN—a moment he saw as the capstone to years of work—he was quieter than ever, thanks, he claims, to a moment he shared with his dying mother in 2014. "There are very few times in life when I feel like someone told me something that was meant for that moment. I just found a recording of something my mom told me before she died at the last family dinner we had. She said, 'Roy, sometimes you just have to be still.' So when all that was going on and I had parents on the team responding and Peterson and the coaches, I just didn't say anything."

For the players, it was hard to not read everything that was being written. "It was sort of, 'What's next?'" Jackson recalled. He watched the story evolve from "Who is Roy Johnson" to "What is Bishop Sycamore?" He and his teammates saw former NFL athletes, celebrities, and even politicians posting about the controversy. Once again, *Last Chance U* was being referenced—but this time it was new rumored interest from production companies and Johnson "still trying to set something up." And then the first of the team's remaining opponents canceled their upcoming game. "It was like 'Dang, who else is going to cancel?'" Within days, the answer was "all of them." By the end of the week, Bishop Sycamore didn't have a schedule. Jackson and his teammates had gone from ESPN to the end of their season. "It definitely felt unfair."

It felt unfair to Johnson, too. In a rare moment of empathy, Johnson admitted that the outcome made him question things. Although he doesn't feel bad about many of the positions he put Bishop Sycamore players in, he does feel bad that they had most of a season taken from them. "All the kids from this year, this specific year, they took the worst loss," he said. "They didn't even get to finish their season. All the other kids can talk all the shit they want, but the reality is if we sit down with and have a conversation, they could never win. Because the reality is: Where's your transcripts? Did you go to class? Did you go online like we told you to go online? Did you do what you were supposed to do? Did you register with the NCAA? Did you pay your registration fee? Did you do any of that? Okay, you didn't do any of that. So you can't tell me it's my fault that you didn't go to college."

As he watched the news cycle unfold, Johnson felt confused. In his view, he hadn't done anything different than dozens of other schools. His only regret, he said, was not speaking up when games started being canceled. "I wish I would have fought more to keep the games on the schedule, because that ended up affecting them. But I'm also not upset with the fact that I took my mom's advice and just stayed still. People aren't going to understand me; they're not going to understand Bishop Sycamore. They don't care to understand it." The least of his crimes, as he saw it, was losing badly to IMG Academy. "How exactly did we dupe ESPN? It's because we got beat," he said. "Here's the funny thing about it: We got beat 58–0, right? The very next week, LaSalle—perennial state champion in Ohio—got beat 58–7. So what you're saying is, my school is as good as LaSalle, who has a $15 or 20 million endowment fund?"

In Johnson's view, he and his team were simply doing what they had to. To him, the high school football climate necessitates that kind of unscrupulousness, and he feels confident that he and his programs are no worse than dozens of other schools in America. "One of the things people don't seem to understand—whether they like it or not—is that the disparity between the top and the bottom in high school football is no different than the disparity in college football. You're always going to have Ohio States who are going to play Youngstown State. Youngstown State or Miami of Ohio are always going to take that million-dollar check. They'll take it every time. Think about this perspective of it: There are 300 or 400 [prep schools] and all of them have fifth-year seniors. The whole East Coast is littered with them.... They all do the same thing. There wasn't really any difference between us and them.... If this was a private White school, nobody would have said anything."

As willing as he is to point out Johnson's lies, the comparison to other schools is where Hall agrees. A veteran of the youth sports world, he's no stranger to blowouts, and he's no stranger to the business of sports. What he saw when he looked at this version of Bishop Sycamore was a program doing things the wrong way, but aiming for the same things other schools do. And unlike many of those other schools, he points out, Bishop Sycamore was a program run by Black founders, administrators, and coaches. And to admit that they're doing something similar to other schools would be an uncomfortable truth.

"People don't like mirrors," Hall said. "If you admit, 'Yeah, we scheduled them; we put them on our schedule,' then you too arc admitting that you understood what it was about. Or you are also admitting that maybe it's not as bad as the media is portraying it to be. It was just a bunch of guys trying to do something who just couldn't get the funding to do it. There are a couple perspectives that you can have about it. The whole Bishop Sycamore thing, to my knowledge, blew up for a few reasons. But it blew up because Roy Johnson's a salesman and he embellished about things that he should not have embellished about."

"For me, it's just simple facts," Johnson said. "What facts were presented that we were wrong? What didn't we do right? Nothing."

12

NON-BINDING OFFERS

From Roy Johnson's perspective, the trials and tribulations of the COF Academy and Bishop Sycamore projects were always worth the trouble because their goals were always genuine: he wanted to get kids to college.

No matter the corners he cut or the people he angered or the blowout defeats he suffered, Johnson remained steadfast that his ultimate goal was to create a pathway to college for kids who had no path. He had connections, he had experience in the football world, he had coaches who knew what they were doing. At least, in his view. He didn't always know what he was doing on the organizational side of the program, but he believed, from day one, that he knew how to get college scholarship offers, and he told anyone who would listen.

Offensive lineman Savior Conley was one of many players drawn to the newly formed COF Academy program for exactly that reason. Conley had already graduated high school, but wanted to improve his GPA to qualify for scholarships. He told *Pressd* magazine that the recruiting chances promised by Johnson were the entire reason for him to attend COF Academy.

"This was an opportunity for me to get film for people to see me play. He sold me a dream that different scouts would come to look at me and that I could be on the next level of football. But I didn't talk to no scouts, and I was the only player he was begging to play every game, on both sides of the ball."

Conley dreamt of going to Florida State. He told *Pressd* that Johnson made him believe that goal was within reach. "I'm thinking I can make it, work my hardest, do what I've got to do and make it out of there and get an opportunity to better myself and my life. But going toward the last game, I'm like 'This whole season we haven't been to school. This whole season we haven't seen no scouts.'"

When he left the program, Conley said Johnson called him and told him he was being kicked out. After telling his friends and family what had happened, they called Johnson, who told them that Conley needed to come get his things and leave.

For Johnson, stories like Conley's—players who didn't succeed in getting the offers he promised—come down to a lack of discipline, character, or ability. They were never failures on his part.

Amid the media swirl of the post–Bishop Sycamore years, Johnson admitted to lying on a variety of occasions. He admitted to having regrets, misleading people, failing the kids at some stages, and doing things the wrong way. But through it all, he remained certain that he had been truthful about the doors he was opening for his players.

"I didn't lie about DI offers."

When a layperson hears that a player has received a scholarship offer from a university, it's easy to assume that an "offer" means that school has given the player a chance to play football for that university under scholarship. Unfortunately for high school athletes and their families, that's not always the case.

Ryan Wright is a national recruiting analyst for Rivals, spending most of his year entrenched in the high school football recruiting landscape. He said the biggest misconception he hears about recruiting is when people tell him he should have a player rated higher because of an offer they received from a high-profile school.

"That goes without understanding the player or how the offer came to that person or the timing of the offer, and that offer can become meaningless down the line—especially for a quarterback—if that program already has a quarterback committed," he said. "Just because a player had an offer from a Top 20 program doesn't mean that person is still valued at that level by that school, and it gives no indication of how that kid has continued to evolve and get better over time."

The phrase "an offer" is a nebulous designation that, in practice, means almost nothing.

Players can receive an offer from a school simply for attending a camp and doing well. In an instance like that, a student in the ninth grade can get an offer simply because the school acknowledges that he has potential—they want to keep an eye on him. An assistant coach or even a trainer can make an offer to a player they build a relationship with on the recruiting trail or watch for an impressive performance. One coach might ask a friend on a coaching staff for a favor: "Offer this kid to help boost his recruiting portfolio." These are all versions of offers that sound great and look nice on paper, but come with no binding agreement and ultimately carry very little weight. The final scenario is a concrete offer referred to as "committable." When a player receives this kind of offer, they can commit on the spot if they'd like.

How can a player or his family tell the difference between these offers?

They can't.

"An offer can be two things. It can be a notice of one's skills and potential, depending on where they're at in the recruiting process or in high school, or it can mean, 'We're here to recruit you and we want you to be part of our recruiting class.' At a fundamental level, those are the two different forms of an offer," Wright said.

"It's upon the player, the parent, the guardian, the coach, the trainer—whoever is within the circle of that child—to ask questions. What does this offer mean? Does it mean I can commit and play for your program? The questions need to follow, because it's a non-binding verbal offer for a scholarship, but that doesn't mean the program or the coach needs to adhere to the quote-unquote offer."

For those who look upon high school athletics with a critical eye, it's easy to see why this process and its lack of transparency puts children and families at risk. Tyrre Burks of Players Health often advises young athletes, including his own son, and their families, and said he too often sees talk of "offers" being thrown around without meaning—and sometimes with underhanded intentions.

"The way that the whole program works is that you have a guy who has a ton of relationships with college coaches. Maybe this year, he has three really good athletes and two on the bubble—five athletes with the possibility of playing at the next level. Let's say he has one guy who can play DI and the rest are on the bubble. He's trading and he's going to bargain with that one.

"He's saying, 'I know you want Tyrre, but in order for you to get him, I need you to offer Marcus.' It's called a contingent offer; it's not a real offer, it's a verbal offer. And so the athlete has to say, 'Yes, I want that offer' and commit, and when they commit, the school has to accept that commitment. That's where the offer really comes in. I can verbally give you an offer, but when I say that, you're going to post on social media, 'The University of Illinois offered me,' but it's not a real offer until they accept your commitment, and that's contingent on whether they have the spot available. A lot of high school coaches are using that in their favor. They'll have one athlete who's really good, and get other schools to offer two other athletes to build momentum with the hope that one of those schools actually accepts that commitment and offers them a scholarship. If that happens enough, any kid in the city knows that coach gets kids offers, even though none of those offers are real. So you start to see kids move to other schools and be part of that organization with the promise that they'll get an offer. Then, when they get a verbal offer, they think it's real and they try to get a commitment but they don't actually have an offer. Then they end up in junior college."

Though he's hesitant to call that kind of behavior widespread, Wright also knows plenty of "offers" are given under circumstances that don't reflect football ability or an eventual concrete scholarship. He said he's seen coaches recruit an older brother or even a twin by tossing an offer to their less-talented brother as a way to earn good favor. He's also seen what the recruiting world calls a "buddy offer."

"That's where there's some gray area with everything," he said. "For example, if a Power Five program is really going after one kid … they'll say, 'If it helps, we'll bring your buddy along.'"

The process doesn't just mean kids and families are let down when offers evaporate. Burks recalled mentoring one student who was so thrilled to receive an offer he and his mother agreed to go on an out-of-town campus visit that wasn't paid for. Players Health helps fund trips like those, but Burks knew that the trip was an ill-fated one.

"He was talking to one of the coaches at Oregon, who supposedly offered him. But if you go on an official visit, your travel to the visit is paid for. His visit wasn't. So it wasn't an official visit, but [he] got an offer. They found out at the last minute and still wanted to go out and meet the coach, so we gave them a microgrant to fly out there. But when they got out there, they found out that the offer wasn't legit. And of course, he's now mad at the coach."

How can students and parents navigate these murky waters, and what can be done to prevent kids from being taken advantage of in a recruiting scheme? "It really comes down to educating parents," Burks said. "I'm mentoring a three-star athlete out of Chicago who has about 17 offers, and right now he's finding out that only two of the offers are real. I had a really tough conversation with him and his mom a few weeks ago and I told him, 'You may not want to hear this, but you need to accept those offers immediately.' I told him how to test it out. You call the coach at the school who gave you the offer and say, 'Coach, if I were to commit tomorrow, would you accept my commitment?' If that coach wavers in any way, it's not a real offer."

Wright agrees that the only way to ensure the veracity of a concrete offer is to ask questions. His three suggestions are: Is this a committable offer? How many other players at this position have you offered already? How many players within this class are you taking at my son's position?

As he watches the process play out with the next generation, Burks often thinks about the advantages he can provide his own son thanks to his experience and knowledge. And he knows not everyone else is in such a fortunate position.

"His path is so clear because I've gone through it and I've been educated and I live in this space. For a parent who doesn't know and maybe didn't go to college or even finish high school, that parent doesn't know what to look for. They can be just as naive as the kids in that moment and go, 'This is your shot. You've got to do it.' We have to educate parents about what the process looks like, what a real organization is, what good and bad organizations look like and key questions to ask coaches and other players."

Johnson claims he's seen reports suggesting he inflated the number of kids who had parlayed COF Academy and Bishop Sycamore seasons into offers, and he takes offense at that. "I said 'several.' What does 'several' mean to you? Six-plus? When I think 'several' I think seven." To back up his claim, Johnson offers a variety of names. He said interviewers didn't talk to "the guys who went through the program and went to college. For free."

In Johnson's view, those interviewers are "only talking to the three or four assholes who were around for a week or two and didn't like the program and left or got kicked off the team because they stole TVs, committed armed robbery, whatever dumb shit they did. So we had to kick them off the team. These are the guys who are telling you stuff and then you look at their Instagram and they've got guns pointed."

How much success did Johnson's alleged offers bring to the students at COF Academy and Bishop Sycamore? The picture is bleak. Looking at the players Johnson named on the 2020 and 2021 Bishop Sycamore rosters as evidence of successful college offers, none had the type of success that Johnson promised. Some had no success at all.

Jeremy Naborne, one of the players Johnson assured had a DI offer, ended up playing football at the University of Fort Lauderdale. The program was not sanctioned by the NCAA, and canceled their season after one game in 2022. The address for the school is a strip mall. On social media, players discussed sleeping on air mattresses in abandoned apartments. It was Bishop Sycamore all over again. Armon Scott was previously committed to playing football for the University of Kentucky, a DI SEC school, in 2020. He could've been on the field for a legitimate college program in 2021, but his grades prevented him from playing, and he ended up at Bishop Sycamore instead. The internet rumored that he received an offer from Syracuse in the summer of 2021 before the Bishop Sycamore season, but he did not go on to play for Syracuse. Scott is active on social media, and does not mention playing football anywhere, or being in college at all. Andrew Price and Jordell Smith are also active on social media with no mention of playing college football or attending college.

Girardo Delagatti played for Bishop Sycamore in 2020. He would go on to play football for Ithaca, a Division III college, in 2022, but only after he went back to his original high school, Malverne, after a year at Bishop Sycamore. Any success he had as a player would be more fairly attributed to Malverne, not Johnson or Bishop Sycamore. But even then, his success is limited. Delagatti played in just one game for Ithaca, and as a Division III school, they are prohibited from offering athletic scholarships due to NCAA regulations. Donovan McLendon listed on his social media that he played football at Butler Community College, a far cry from a DI program. However, he does not appear on Butler's football roster for the 2022 season.

Justin Daniel said on social media that he attended Garden City Community College, but he does not appear on their 2022 football roster. Chamor Price claimed on social media that he committed to play at Hutchinson Community College, but did not appear on their 2022 football roster. Greg Sullivan-Crockett played for Johnson every year, from COF Academy all the way through the final year at Bishop Sycamore. He listed on social media that he plays football for Alderson Broaddus University, the same school that former COF Academy coach Ulysses Hall went on to coach for. They are a DII school, and can offer athletic scholarships. However, Sullivan-Crockett was listed on the roster as an unnumbered walk-on player. He did not play in any games for the team in the 2022 season. The odds of a player who played in zero games doing so on an athletic scholarship are slim.

Some other players that Johnson did not tout by name but appeared on a 2021 roster for Bishop Sycamore have similar stories. Jailen Knight went on to Langston University, which plays in the NAIA, lower than the three NCAA divisions. He was listed on their football roster in 2022, but did not appear in any games. Kyle Miller went on to play at Long Beach City College, a community college that plays in a conference with other community colleges and is lower in the rankings than the NCAA or NAIA. There are no known players at the NCAA Division I level to have played for Johnson at COF

Academy or Bishop Sycamore. Even if a Bishop Sycamore player had been talented and educationally qualified enough, that player likely wouldn't have been eligible to play college football at all. The NCAA has an online eligibility center, meant to provide parents and students a method to check to ensure that the programs in which they are enrolled will indeed help them play at the next level. An account status of "cleared" means the program meets NCAA eligibility requirements. Bishop Sycamore never left the "in review" stage of those requirements. As early as August of 2020, Bishop Sycamore's status was listed as "in review," and it remains in that status to this day. The NCAA eligibility center says that for schools in review, their "courses and proof of graduation may not be used in the eligibility certification process."

At least one player took a reverse path, going from a college to Bishop Sycamore. Mecose Todd was on the roster provided to ESPN from the school ahead of their matchup against IMG. But the year prior, he had played college football for Iowa Western Community College. The college's website even lists him as a sophomore. Yet, in spite of playing a year of college football, he was back playing high school football a year later. Although they reside in the tier below the NCAA level that many players aspire to, Iowa Western is a successful program. They play in the first division of the National Junior College Athletic Association and were the football champions in 2012. Six players have played for Iowa Western and gone on to sign with an NFL team. Todd left that program for one that promised the world, even if it was a step backward. Johnson's stated goal of helping players reach the next level was now actively hindering efforts which were already more successful.

Players involved in the programs, like Bishop Sycamore receiver and cornerback Devante Jackson, never saw much evidence of success beyond empty "offers." He remembers after the IMG game, one player—who Jackson noted didn't even score the lone Bishop Sycamore touchdown in that game—got six offers simply from being on television. Jackson couldn't even remember his name. But those rarely panned out, he said, and he knew many players who regretted passing up existing chances at higher education for the prospects of further glory.

"There's people on our team saying they had offers—they probably did have offers … but nobody never knew besides those players," he said. "It was like people gave up their opportunities to go to a juco, a DII, DIII, DI, whatever they had going on, to come to a school to play, to come back to high school—or whatever you wanna call it—to play again."

13

THIS MAN IS INCREDIBLE TELEVISION

The immediate aftermath of the ESPN game was a feeding frenzy that began in Ohio and spread across the country. Between social media users, reporters, and the entertainment industry, everyone wanted a piece of the Bishop Sycamore story. Before the game had even finished, reporters were calling ESPN officials, digging up stories about COF Academy, and trying to learn more about Roy Johnson, whose on-screen appearance blasting a water bottle into his mouth became etched into social media history. Parody accounts and websites made jokes about the school. On August 30, the day after the game, "Bishop Sycamore" was the number one trending topic on Twitter in the United States. And behind the scenes, filmmakers and production studios scrambled to capitalize on the story that had captured the public eye. It had taken a nationally televised game to bring Roy Johnson and his football team into the limelight, and now everyone was looking.

Beginning as early as the second half, Ben Koo knew that the story was something special. Koo knew that the topic was perfect for his blog, *Awful Announcing*, which often offers a meta look at the business of sports media. At first, he thought the story was just that—a sports media story. But the more he looked into Bishop Sycamore, their history, and the characters involved, the more he felt like he was uncovering something. "I'm not buying it," became his refrain about all things Bishop Sycamore, and as he posted stories, his audience backed up his hunch that people were interested. "Everyone was dropping nuggets on Twitter, and then I put together like five or six things and added five to six of my own, and then the big story drops and we get a ton of traffic."

The first *Awful Announcing* story on Bishop Sycamore earned more than 30 times the traffic of an average article. "People were getting really into it," so Koo kept dumping time into the story. Between August 29 and September 2, *Awful Announcing* posted 11 stories related to Bishop Sycamore, almost all thanks to Koo. "This is my routine for the next few days: Work, work, work, work, get in bed with my girlfriend and tell her I'm going to sleep, and then I'm on my phone for four more hours DMing people, giving info, looking over things, going to bed at 3:00 or 4:00 AM and waking up at 7:00."

In the early days of COF Academy and again when Bishop Sycamore reemerged from the ashes of its predecessor, OHSAA officials and others had informed Ohio news outlets of the story, including the *Columbus Dispatch*, the *Cleveland Plain-Dealer*, and the *Cincinnati Enquirer*.

They even had the chance to catch on to the story when *Sports Illustrated* tweeted about Bishop Sycamore in 2020, showing highlights of then-quarterback Josh Bogan taking snaps and also playing linebacker. Listed at 6'2", 240 pounds, Bogan stood out. But nothing in the highlights detailed anything about the Bishop Sycamore program, and no one asked why Bogan was still playing high school athletics in 2020 when he had graduated from Michigan's South Lake High School in 2019. No one followed up in 2021, when he was playing at Hocking College, a community college in Nelsonville, Ohio, with an undergraduate student body of around 3,400—a far cry from the DI destinations that Bishop Sycamore promised.

But now that the story was spreading like wildfire, traditional print media was playing catch-up. All three of Ohio's biggest papers covered the story, and followed their coverage with opinion pieces on what Bishop Sycamore had done. The *Plain-Dealer* ran a headline that said, "Bishop Sycamore should be avoided by all high school football programs." The *Dispatch* admitted that, "sadly, the Bishop Sycamore scheme was not a secret around here." Columnist Paul Daugherty mocked Bishop Sycamore parents in the *Enquirer* in his snarky piece, "Calling BS on Bishop Sycamore Football." All three papers had been alerted to Bishop Sycamore and COF Academy as early as the summer of 2018.

Even the local TV stations got involved, drawing Jay Richardson back into the picture. It had been reported that Richardson was listed as the superintendent of COF Academy, so when the feeding frenzy of 2021 began, questions were asked of the former Buckeye and ABC6/FOX28 football analyst. To dispel questions linking him to Bishop Sycamore, ABC6 interviewed him on their own website, allowing him to defend himself. "My legal team is working to get my name removed from this. I have not signed any documents, no involvement with that particularly other than trying to help the school get resources at one point. And once I realized that it just wasn't going to be possible, I said, 'Hey look I can't help out,'" Richardson told his own news team. He would continue to deny all involvement, claiming he was involved in the lawsuits because "they probably see an opportunity to involve someone that they feel like could help them recoup some of those funds."

Despite those denials, Richardson was listed as the superintendent of COF Academy in their official filing with the ODE. A letter included with the filing read:

> "It's time for a TRANSFORMATIVE paradigm of PRE-COLLEGE PREPARATION for AN INCREASINGLY SOCIO-ECONOMIC DIVERSE POPULATION. Conventional models, while still solid, are no longer up

to the heightened challenges of the present. Exponentially improving READINESS OF aspiring and gifted students TO MEET THE HEAVY DEMANDS OF TRADITIONAL COLLEGE PARTICIPATION has created a TRANSFORMATIVE EDUCATION OPPORTUNITY. The key development is THE DRAMATIC INTEREST OF TWO OF THE LARGEST AFRICAN AMERICAN RELIGIOUS COMMUNITIES TO COME TOGETHER because they see the NEED TO INTEGRATE THEIR THINKING AND SUPPORT around a holistic view of non-traditional college preparation to educate America's future leaders.

We believe that God's Word is the bible. We believe in teaching this through the interpretation guided by the sub doctrine of the African Methodist church, Baptist church, and Plymouth Brethren.

We believe that there are many lessons and values in the Bible that are applicable to today's world and more importantly applicable in the lives of young adults.

We believe in focusing on what the Bible says about love, patience, and accountability.

We believe that these lessons that are in the bible can help mold young individuals and prepare them for the world they are going to be a part of help mold.

We believe that everyone should have a right to a good education.

> We believe that we are to give as many young men and women a chance to be a better person through values, morals, and education.
>
> We believe that this school will give these young and men this opportunity because we are COF.... Christians of Faith."

The letter is signed "Jay Richardson, Superintendent."

As reporters, producers, and filmmakers scrambled and raced to find information on what they perceived to be a brand new story, they would eventually come to the same conclusion as many researchers before them: the internet knew about this story all along. Yappi is a niche message board site dedicated to Ohio high school sports. The board's header describes Yappi as "a site dedicated to bringing you news, information, and forums for high school sports in Ohio." Populated by some of the most die-hard high school sports fans in the state, every game can be fodder for an argument on Yappi, and wild opinions and conspiracy theories run rampant. But from nearly the beginning of this story, Yappi users agreed on one thing: COF Academy and Bishop Sycamore were a scam.

Tim Taylor founded Yappi in 2001. Running the website is his full-time job. He recalls users having all of the information on Bishop Sycamore well before the game on ESPN.

"I remember when they were Christians of Faith back in 2018," Taylor said, "I usually try to stay neutral on the site, but I'm someone who doesn't favor these types of programs. I like kids to go to school where they go to school, play sports for their school, and these fake schools that are popping up, I'm not a big fan of. So when I saw a thread on this type of thing pop up, I always made sure to follow it and participate. COF Academy and Bishop Sycamore were the biggest general interest threads. The whole state was interested in it, and people from outside the state as well. We had people coming in from different forums, different Twitter accounts, and Facebook to read what was posted on here. They knew how detailed the people were investigating it. These people were well-versed in what was going on."

On June 8, 2018, the first mention of COF Academy appeared on Yappi with the headline "COF Academy? Are they real?" Before the school year even began, the fans that dominated Yappi knew something was fishy. "If they're not [real], they've sure fooled some ADs," said a poster using the name "sapiential et veritas." "Relatively respectful people are associated with them and have updated their LinkedIn pages to say so. Neither Google nor the Franklin County Auditor nor the Department of Education nor the Secretary of State nor anybody has ever heard of them. Are they for real?"

While Johnson tried to keep his roster a secret, posters found the names and graduating years of the players, disproving the claim that everyone was in high school. Posters would continue to follow the saga over the years. In February of 2019, well ahead of Bishop Sycamore's first season, Yappi users were already calling them out. "Looks just like COF," said one user. "School must have begun. Where are they located? Do they still have a hypothetical campus?" Users of an online message board were asking questions that Bishop Sycamore opponents were uninterested in. "This is literally the same exact thread as last year except with a different name for the school. I honestly can't believe that these scam artists are ballsy enough to keep up their schtick. Even more unbelievable is that anyone would even entertains the idea of sending their kids there," said one poster.

Peterson himself joined the message board, posting under the name GodsChild86 to try to defend Bishop Sycamore. In April of 2019, he said:

> "It's funny that there are people in this world that live to criticize something new.... well ... yes we have building ... yes we have a team ... yes we have a schedule ... yes we have teachers.... yes we have a board ... yes we have an educational program. So you can be negative all you want.... but our light will outshine your darkness!!! Be

> blessed…" Peterson never registered Bishop Sycamore as a school in the 2019 school year. "Honestly…. we are not operating under a cloud of secrecy. We have just chosen to not release anything until every I is dotted and every t is crossed … This is not even the same group that was running COF. The young men and their families are fully aware of what we offer with full disclosure. We are doing something that Columbus and Central Ohio will be proud of. And if you don't agree with what we are doing…. if you think or even hope we fail … then you should just have a seat because we are going to be here for a while…"

He would also defend his background and his own legal issues by comparing himself to Donald Trump on the message board. "When you look at President Trump, do you look at a person who has started businesses that have failed, a person who has filed bankruptcy 6 or 7 times, or a great businessman?" he argued.

In July of 2021, users took note of the IMG matchup on ESPN and its scheduling just two days after the game against Sto-Rox. One user commented, "Hold up. These clowns got ESPN to agree to televise one of their games? Never once did anyone from ESPN think to themselves 'Maybe we should check to see if this is a real school.'" ESPN executives would later claim they were unaware of the game occurring just days before the one they televised, but the information was readily available to anyone who was willing to look. And although Peterson and Johnson jumped into message board conversations to defend themselves at various times, no one defended Bishop Sycamore harder than Maimone, who posted on Yappi under the name "Jersey Flyer."

"All 113 players currently rostered attend classes online/in-person Mon-Fri," Maimone wrote on August 8. When another poster claimed that none of Bishop Sycamore's players were actually in high school. "The school is situated in the Easton section of Columbus. There are two structures comprised of living quarters, classrooms, a weight room, and three indoor practice fields," Maimone claimed. All of his statements were easily disproved. Even after the fallout, Maimone refused to admit he ever lied, posting on the website in December of 2021, "Duke Men's Lacrosse, Nicholas Sandmann, Kyle Rittenhouse, Bishop Sycamore football. Who's next? #rushtojudgement #fantasticlies #LastChanceHigh."

Multiple news outlets cited the website in the weeks following the IMG game. "This is my lifelong project. It is a business, but it's my baby. It was neat to see it getting some press that I think is well deserved," Taylor said. "The people who are on the site are that interesting, and they know that much stuff, and they deserve to be recognized for all the stuff they do. It's amazing how much great stuff comes from these people. They deserve this recognition." With all the information readily available, why didn't more people seek out the information on COF Academy and Bishop Sycamore? "I think the schools needed games. This was a team that was willing to come play you instead of having to drive to Michigan or Pennsylvania. This was a school that was willing to play you wherever you are," Taylor said, "No one was really that worried about it."

Amid the swirl of news, Bishop Sycamore officials sought to course correct the narrative through local TV media. NBC4 interviewed coach Tyren Jackson, briefly described as "the new head coach of Bishop Sycamore" for a conversation that seemed designed to drag headlines back in their favor. "We do not offer curriculum," Jackson admitted, before adding the baffling claim that, "We are not a school. That's not what Bishop Sycamore is, and I think that's what the biggest misconception about us was, and that was our fault. Because that was a mistake on paperwork." Jackson even tried to capitalize on the omnipresence of the story. "Once the smoke clears, we're national news," he said. "Whoever does schedule us next will be national news."

Columbus Dispatch reporter Bailey Johnson had only been on the high school football beat for about six months, and planned to spend her Sunday doing anything other than working. Until that day, she didn't know anything about

Bishop Sycamore other than one mention that had come from the newsroom a few months earlier. In May, she said, a colleague on the *Dispatch*'s education beat had passed along a call from a concerned parent who reached out wondering about a school called Bishop Sycamore that they struggled to find information on. The parent wondered if anyone at the *Dispatch* had been aware of them. When the note was passed along to the sports department, no one had any idea.

"When the game was on ESPN, I was like, 'Oh my god,'" Johnson said, quickly realizing that her weekend was over. "The game was on a Sunday, so in my head, I was like, 'Okay, I'll start looking at this Monday morning.' But I couldn't—I had to start working on it on Sunday because it was exploding so much that we had to get working on it right away." Fellow Gannett publication *USA Today* picked up Johnson's early coverage and the story got about 100,000 page views in its first few days online, a number that blew her away. Soon, other national publications were on the story—the *Washington Post*, *The Athletic*, the *New York Times*, and *Sports Illustrated* all ran stories, while YouTube personalities and international newspapers created yet another news cycle—and she was making appearances on *The Dan Patrick Show*, ESPN's *Outside the Lines*, a financial network called Cheddar News, a New Zealand radio show, and TSN in Canada. "It was completely surreal. I don't know that I'll ever forget the feeling of seeing the little email preview pop up in the corner of my screen and having it be someone from ESPN PR trying to set that up. It was absolutely insane."

The *Dispatch* wrote several articles and columns covering the story, but across town, Koo's work dwarfed the paper's. Working day and night, his coverage increased in depth—and palpable disdain for the program—by the article. Headlines like "ESPN's announcers spent a lot of the IMG-Bishop Sycamore HS blowout criticizing Bishop Sycamore's selection for it" quickly shifted in tone toward "We learned more about how Bishop Sycamore ended up playing on ESPN, and it's only getting shadier." Admittedly, he had become a bit obsessed, and it's because he found the story so intriguing as it moved from a funny pop culture moment into the territory of something that seemed more sinister. "I'm like, 'This is kind of funny that they pulled this over on ESPN,'" he thought, until he dug deeper. "But there's a serious component to this. It's not just funny that ESPN got duped. There's some dicey shit that I'm motivated to get into."

Within days of the game, Koo decided he could do something more substantial with the Bishop Sycamore story than just publishing some articles. He had no experience, but had always wanted to make a documentary, so when he got an email from superstar comedian Kevin Hart's production company, he thought it was his chance. "Then I got hit up by two or three more agents, a couple production companies, and I thought, 'This is fucking nuts.'" He hired an agent and began learning how to navigate the process, but he wasn't the only one. By early September, Hart's production company with NBA agent and marketing mogul Rich Paul, former NFL player and *Good Morning America* host Michael Strahan, and *The Athletic* all made public announcements that they intended to create documentary projects around the story. "As soon as I started following this story, I was immediately drawn to it and knew it was something that myself and my team at HartBeat had to dive into. HBP thrives in the doc-series space," Hart told *Deadline*. "We understand how to break down stories and capture the most interesting and honest moments in a narrative. We know this con comes with a robust backstory and cannot wait to share it with the world."

The race heated up when Strahan's production company, SMAC Entertainment, signed Roy Johnson himself, agreeing to pay him an unknown amount for the rights to his life story and his participation in their documentary, *BS High*. "To secure the rights to Roy's story as the head coach of the Bishop Sycamore High School football team that has gone viral and made national headlines is incredible, especially as it plays out in real time," said Constance Schwartz-Morini, who founded SMAC Entertainment with Strahan. "When our head of unscripted, Ethan Lewis, brought this story to Michael and my attention, we knew we could tell it with the gravitas, authenticity, and journalistic integrity that it deserves." SMAC was the most prompt in finding a distributor for their project, signing a deal with HBO less than two months after the ESPN game.

The media churn made things challenging for Koo, who didn't have a household name, the backing of a major production company, or a distributor for his project. "When anything viral happens, everyone comes in," he said. "There's ambulance-chasing for these things. It makes the product worse because people are attached to different things. You have players who do not want to be in the project with Roy. The agencies really get into this. Anyone who isn't involved in your project shit talks [the others]. I was totally unprepared for the element of fending off multiple fronts for access. You have *Complex*, *The Athletic*, *Awful Announcing* all claiming to have the knowledge of what's going on in the story. In today's world, you need celebrity power … if you're not cognizant of what people are angling at, you'll get crushed as this thing goes along." Koo kept plugging away for months, convincing both Johnson and Andre Peterson to film with him. But eventually he came to terms with how unlikely the project seemed, and by late 2022, only the Strahan and HBO project remained.

To helm that project, SMAC reached out to Martin Desmond Roe, a British filmmaker who had directed the documentary miniseries *Wiz Khalifa: Behind the Cam* for the production company. He had recently partnered to form a directing duo with fellow director Travon Free, who had a background playing high school football that helped the story catch his eye. The pair were an accomplished team to helm the film. One of their projects, a 2020 short film called *Two Distant Strangers*, which Free wrote and the duo directed, won the award for Best Live Action Short Film at the 93rd Academy Awards. At first, Roe was unsure about the project and its scope, but after interacting with Johnson, he was sold.

"We got on the phone with Roy and we were like, 'This guy is incredible. We've got to see if there was a story here.' The football story of it is interesting. But different mediums have different requirements, and to make a compelling documentary you need compelling subjects. And I think a lot of the time with these, 'Ripped from the headlines' stories, the people are just regular people. They get a little overwhelmed by the spotlight, if you will. It doesn't necessarily turn into a great documentary. But we spoke to Roy and I was like, 'Oh my gosh. This man is incredible television.' We had to give him a platform to say his piece. He has so much to say."

With the documentary in place and the buzz dying down, the frenzy was gone as quick as it had come. A few weeks after the ESPN game, Bishop Sycamore had faded from the public eye. *Awful Announcing* kept an eye on the story, but Koo watched interest dissipate even in the community where the story was based. To him, the overarching theme of Bishop Sycamore's news cycle was a failure in Columbus' local media, where Gannett's ownership of the *Columbus Dispatch* and affiliate papers has meant layoffs and a variety of shuttered publications—including *ThisWeek News*, who broke the COF Academy story—and a lack of both willingness and manpower to track a story as large and challenging as the Bishop Sycamore saga. "I did a lot of national interviews, and nothing for local Columbus," he said. "Who can we say made any contribution to any reporting on that story from Columbus local media? I saw a YouTuber bring two guys in from the original team. The *Dispatch* was bad. Local TV just did their 90-second things. There just aren't that many investigative resources out there, and when you're late you're late.... Columbus media is just not particularly strong. The *Dispatch* never gets in on these stories and they never move the ball at all."

Even after missing the story once before, local media simply lost interest, including Bailey Johnson. "I thought it would be something that I would continue to work on in the background, but at this point we're almost a year later and it's not even circulating anymore. It's just one of those things like, 'Remember that crazy thing that happened last year?' I think it speaks to Bishop Sycamore's ability to just kind of disappear. We followed it through for a couple weeks and they got a new coach and they were still trying to schedule games, and by the time they couldn't find anybody to play, it just kind of all fizzled out. There's not a whole lot of public records or anything to dig up. That's how stories get staying power—you keep following through on records searches or court cases happening. But this can just kind of go away."

14

IF IT'S A SCAM, I'M LITERALLY SCAMMING MYSELF

The IMG game gave Bishop Sycamore worldwide notoriety, but in order to hold them accountable for any of the variety of bad, illegal, or unethical decisions they made, the program's home state of Ohio would need to lead the way. Just two days after the ESPN game, governor Mike DeWine felt the pressure to act, and let the country know that he had taken note of the situation.

"Like many Ohioans, I am concerned by the recent reports and questions raised about Bishop Sycamore. While this weekend's football game brought concerns about the health and safety of players, it also raised red flags about the school's operations. Schools like Bishop Sycamore have an obligation under Ohio law to meet certain minimum standards. Whether Bishop Sycamore meets these standards is not clear. I have asked the Ohio Department of Education (ODE) to conduct an investigation into Bishop Sycamore to ensure compliance with Ohio law and to ensure the school is providing the educational opportunities Ohio students deserve."

Three years earlier, the Ohio Department of Education had already investigated a Roy Johnson–led faux school. Now, they were tasked with investigating yet another one.

The department took its time, using more than three months to complete the investigation, this time under the scrutiny of the entire country rather than a few interested high school football fanatics. So when the report was finally released on December 17, 2021, it garnered plenty of interest. It also confirmed what many knew: "Unfortunately, the facts suggest that Bishop Sycamore High School was and is, in fact, a scam."

The result of the investigation was a blistering 79-page report confirming that Bishop Sycamore did not meet the basic minimum standards of a school. The report was critical of nearly every element of the Bishop Sycamore program.

"All students should receive a quality education," said interim state superintendent of public instruction Stephanie Siddens in a statement. "Anytime students fail to receive the quality education they need and deserve, we want to fully investigate the situation to learn what we can do to prevent it from happening ever again. In light of what we've learned about Bishop Sycamore, we've identified steps we can and will take that we believe will make it more difficult for something like this to reoccur. Our report also includes a wider list of recommendations that, while they will require broader support to implement, could prevent a repeat of Bishop Sycamore entirely. Ultimately, we remain committed to doing everything we can to ensure each of our students is challenged, prepared, and empowered to reach their full potential."

But along with the ODE's scathing language and lengthy explanation of how and why Bishop Sycamore was able to exist came a pair of disheartening revelations: Not only had the State of Ohio been made aware of Bishop Sycamore's dealings and responded by doing nothing, they also still found themselves completely unable to take meaningful action to punish those responsible for the program or prevent them from attempting the same scheme again.

Like COF Academy before it, Bishop Sycamore had eventually filed as a non-chartered, non-tax-supported school. The report confirms, "As a non-chartered, non-tax-supported school, Bishop Sycamore does not have a charter issued by the State Board of Education and does not need approval from the State Board or the Department to operate." However, that recognition meant so little to the school that they did not attempt to register for the 2019–20 season, waiting instead until the 2020–21 school year to seek registration.

The report sought to answer seven questions regarding Bishop Sycamore:

1. What are the truly held religious beliefs that form the school's foundation and hence its alleged non-chartered, non-tax-supported status?
2. Has the school previously operated in a manner to ensure the requisite hours open for instruction with pupils in attendance?

3. To what extent has the school enabled parental reporting of students' enrollment or withdrawal in the school to the treasurer of the respective school districts of residence?
4. To what extent are the requirements for teacher and administrator qualifications verified?
5. To what extent are the required courses of study offered?
6. What are the criteria used to support pupil promotion from grade to grade?
7. Is the school ensuring compliance with appropriate state and local health, fire, and safety laws?

The report unveiled that Bishop Sycamore had been on the radar of the ODE for some time. In August of 2019, when their Daytona Beach matchup in the Freedom Bowl had been canceled due to breach of contract, the *Daytona Beach News-Journal* had contacted the ODE requesting information about Bishop Sycamore.

"Prompted by this inquiry, Sue Cosmo, director of the department's office of nonpublic educational options, directed her staff to attempt to contact the school and identify its address. Staff reported back that there was no phone number or address on the school's website, only vague representation that the school was located between Bexley and Columbus. Staff found that under the 'Students' tab on the school's website to enroll, the user was directed to the EdOptions Virtual School. Department staff contacted EdOptions but was informed that Bishop Sycamore was not a client of the virtual school."

Despite those red flags, the ODE took no action at the time. Months later, Bishop Sycamore finally applied for non-chartered, non-tax-supported status in July of 2020. Because of their repeated instances of failing to provide an address for the school, the ODE did not initially grant Bishop Sycamore their requested status, and it would have to wait until February of 2021 to be listed as a school for the 2020–21 school year. In the interim, parents had to file paperwork stating that they were homeschooling their children so that the minors on the Bishop Sycamore team were not deemed truant. According to the report, the decision to list Bishop Sycamore as a school was met with internal debate. "Staff members continued to express concerns about the school's legitimacy. They also questioned whether the Department had the authority to take any action since the school was representing in its filings that it was following the minimum standards." Put another way, although the employees at the ODE did not *believe* Bishop Sycamore, they also were legally obligated to simply take them at their word. They had no legal authority to do anything else.

Later, Bishop Sycamore would list their school address as the location of Resolute Athletic Complex, a Columbus indoor sports facility that no one could confuse for a school. The complex provides space for a variety of sports, with an emphasis on soccer, and hosts dozens of games on its fields at any given day. A mezzanine area provides friends and family members a place to watch those games. Nothing in the facility appears to even slightly resemble a classroom. But ODE officials visited the space anyway, and "observed the areas of the athletic facility." They also spoke to the facility's director of business development, who told them that Bishop Sycamore "did not rent the facility much over the past year," and had occasionally been there "perhaps monthly based on the weather." That official believed Bishop Sycamore paid less than $1,000 for its total usage of the space, which represented less than 1 percent of its annual usage. She said, "Bishop Sycamore asked about using the mezzanine of the facility, which includes tables and chairs, for a study area for students' use," and said the program "represented that it intended to have a tutor for an hour after workouts, but the school never used the mezzanine for tutoring."

One major element of the report was its investigation into the "truly held beliefs" of Bishop Sycamore's religious element. But even that was a difficult proposition for the investigation because of the existing laws. Instead, all Bishop Sycamore was *really* required to complete in order to certify those beliefs was to check some boxes. "The challenge for the Department in this case is that schools are not required to submit any description of their truly held religious beliefs to the Department.

On the annual certification report for the 2020–2021 school year, Bishop Sycamore checked the box to indicate that the school was 'not chartered or seeking a charter due to truly held religious beliefs.' The school also checked the subsequent box to indicate that it had given written statements of its beliefs to parents. The Department's annual certification report form for the 2021–2022 school year does not include the prompts regarding the school's truly held religious beliefs and its written statement to parents about the beliefs."

Still, they set out to find an answer. But without much information to go on, they simply guessed. They judged the school's religious affiliation on outside appearances, including a January 2021 statement that read, "We are a Christian school so we tell no lie" and Peterson's Twitter profile calling himself a "preacher of the Gospel." Because of the inclusion of "Bishop" at the beginning of the school's name, the ODE even guessed that they were affiliated with the Catholic Church, in spite of their Methodist church connections. "This investigation confirmed that Bishop Sycamore High School is not affiliated with the Catholic Diocese of Columbus. Often, a bishop's name on a private school indicates a Catholic school. The Diocese of Columbus confirmed to the Department that the Diocese has no connection to Bishop Sycamore High School." Eventually, they were simply left stumped due to a "dearth" of information. "Peterson's statements suggest that the school has religious beliefs, but the Department is unable to identify with specificity what those religious beliefs are. And without identifying the school's religious beliefs, the Department could not begin to ascertain whether those religious beliefs are truly held." They did, however, make an attempt to read between the lines with regard to religion: "It appears that Bishop Sycamore does not have truly held religious beliefs that led the school to pursue a course as a non-chartered, non-tax-supported school. It appears instead that Bishop Sycamore took this route because it could become established merely by submitting a form and some accompanying documents. All that was left was to assemble players for the next high school football powerhouse."

The report took note of the way the IMG game and the spotlight had sent Bishop Sycamore leaders scrambling to do damage control. It cited Tyren Jackson's controversial interview in which he claimed that "we are not a school" and blamed the "misconception" on "paperwork issues." Jackson went on to say that Bishop Sycamore would not be seeking any status from the ODE for the 2021–22 school year. Despite that, paperwork was filed on September 30, 2021. The paperwork stated there was a single student enrolled at the school: Javan Peterson, Andre Peterson's son. The address for the school was listed as Peterson's house.

Although multiple requests had been made to Peterson and Johnson for documentation about Bishop Sycamore by this point, the filing did not contain any of the requested information. Instead, Johnson and Peterson requested only to speak with the ODE directly. The ODE agreed and had a conference call with the duo. During that call, "Peterson explained that Bishop Sycamore only had four to five kids in the school and 40 kids on the football team. He said further that some of the kids had four years of football and four years of high school but were not being accepted into colleges because of their grades or 'not being seen by the right people.'" This admission of violation of OHSAA rules, which bars anyone from playing in a fifth year of football or playing football after graduating high school, was in direct contrast to previous statements and contractual commitments Bishop Sycamore had made. Despite being caught in the lie, Johnson and Peterson continued to try to shift blame. "They complained about the OHSAA actions that have kept the team from playing other local high school football teams. They lamented how one football game caused so much damage to their reputation." Peterson and Johnson never provided the documentation that the ODE requested.

During their conversation, Peterson also shared an odd glimpse into how he and the program justified their "religious" status. He said the school "provides religious study," but admitted that study was not reflected on transcripts. He pointed to the name Bishop Sycamore, which he claimed was "influenced by a story from the biblical Gospel of Luke where a man named Zacchaeus climbs a sycamore tree in order to be noticed by Jesus, who was passing through the town." It was Peterson's favorite story in the Bible, and he "explained that the title of Bishop was included in the school's name because it means 'overseer.'" Even the goal of the school reflected Zacchaeus. Peterson told Cosmo that the school "was an attempt at giving students 'the right exposure' so that they are seen by 'the right people' in the same way that 'Zacchaeus was seen by Jesus after climbing the sycamore tree.'"

Ultimately, the final report bluntly answers its seven questions, which dealt with only the 2020–21 and 2021–22 school years because Bishop Sycamore was not filed as a school at all for the 2019–20 year. None of the answers to the department's questions were positive:

1. What are the truly held religious beliefs that form the school's foundation and hence its alleged non-chartered, non-tax-supported status?
   a. The Department is unable to identify with specificity the religious beliefs of Bishop Sycamore High School.
2. Has the school previously operated in a manner to ensure the requisite hours open for instruction with pupils in attendance?
   a. The Department has confirmed the standard was not met for the 2020–2021 school year. The Department

finds that Bishop Sycamore High School was not open for instruction for the requisite hours for the 2020–2021 school year. For the 2021–2022 school year, the Department is unable to confirm whether the school was open for instruction for the requisite hours.

3. To what extent has the school enabled parental reporting of students' enrollment or withdrawal in the school to the treasurer of the respective school districts of residence?
   a. The Department confirmed the standard was not met. The Department finds that students' enrollment in Bishop Sycamore High School was not reported to the treasurer of the respective school districts of residence for the 2020–2021 and the 2021–2022 school year.
4. To what extent are the requirements for teacher and administrator qualifications verified?
   a. The Department is unable to confirm that Bishop Sycamore High School verifies that teachers and administrators meet the requirements.
5. To what extent are the required courses of study offered?
   a. The Department is unable to confirm that Bishop Sycamore offers required courses of study to its students.
6. What are the criteria used to support pupil promotion from grade to grade?
   a. The Department is unable to identify any criteria used by Bishop Sycamore High School to promote students from grade to grade.

7. Is the school ensuring compliance with appropriate state and local health, fire, and safety laws?
    a. The Department is unable to confirm Bishop Sycamore has complied with appropriate health, fire, and safety laws.

The ODE found no evidence that Bishop Sycamore operated as a school in any capacity.

"The public statements about the school have been consistently inconsistent. The current head coach denies Bishop Sycamore's status as a school, then the school files another annual certification with the Department. Peterson was quoted as saying there were around 80 students in the school, yet the school's forms disclose only three students for one year and one student the following year. This pattern of misdirection leaves one concerned about the truth regarding the school's operations. Further, Bishop Sycamore officials were given the opportunity to provide additional information to demonstrate the school's legitimacy and compliance. They declined to do so. Without the clarification from the school to prove its compliance, common sense leads one to the most obvious explanation: Bishop Sycamore is not a school as it purports on paper to be."

But in spite of all those findings, all the black-and-white statements of failure and the clear misrepresentation of the program, any action would be stymied by jurisdiction. Ohio law does not give the ODE the authority to sanction or penalize schools that do not meet the minimum operations standards. And because Bishop Sycamore applied as a non-chartered, non-tax-supported school, there was no charter to revoke. There was no tax money to withhold as punishment. All the ODE could do was simply not include Bishop Sycamore in their annual listing of non-chartered, non-tax-supported schools. The only thing within the power of the ODE was to give recommendations in an effort to ensure that a scheme like the program does not occur again in the future. Those recommendations included consulting with the Ohio attorney general regarding potential legal action against Bishop Sycamore, making a new rule expressly prohibiting non-chartered, non-tax-supported schools from operating unless they are sanctioned by the ODE, and allowing the ODE to fully investigate schools for compliance and not accept them merely at their word.

DeWine appeared to endorse these recommendations after the report was released. In a statement, he said, "This report confirms numerous disturbing allegations regarding Bishop Sycamore. There is no evidence that the 'school' enrolled students this year, had a physical location for classes to meet, employed teachers, nor offered any academic program meeting minimum standards. Ohio families should be able to count on the fact that our schools educate students and don't exist in name only as a vehicle to play high school sports. When an Ohio student goes to school, they deserve a quality education to prepare them for success in the future. I am today asking Attorney General Yost and other offices with jurisdiction to determine whether the alleged deception by Bishop Sycamore violated any civil or criminal laws. I intend to work with the Department of Education and legislative leaders to implement the recommendations contained in this thorough report."

The closing paragraphs in the ODE report drive home why these changes are needed, and who is at fault for Bishop Sycamore. "The recommendations included in this report are presented to help provide potential solutions to the problems revealed in this investigation. The case demonstrates systemic weaknesses … while reform in the oversight of these schools may help in the future, the present situation is a result of the actions of the administrators of Bishop Sycamore High School. In his defense of Bishop Sycamore, Andre Peterson reportedly told *USA Today*: 'If it's a scam, and the kids are not going to school and not doing what they're supposed to do, then I'm literally scamming myself. And more importantly, I'm hurting my own son. So when people say stuff like that … I would literally be taking my son's future and throwing it in the trash.' Unfortunately, the facts suggest that Bishop

Sycamore High School was and is, in fact, a scam … it was a way for students to play football against high school teams and potentially increase students' prospects of playing football at the collegiate level. The cost of this dream for those students wasn't just the tuition charged to attend school. The price was the education the students were entitled to receive.… Education provides an opportunity for each child to achieve their personal ambitions and dreams and to contribute to their neighbors and community. Each child in Ohio is entitled to an education of high quality. That includes the children at Bishop Sycamore. Indeed, each child at Bishop Sycamore deserves better."

With DeWine allegedly on board and recommendations straight from the Department dealing with the issue, how quickly would action follow the report? In fact, nothing has followed the report. Its recommendations have not been followed. There was no follow-up investigation by the Ohio attorney general's office. According to an OAG spokesperson, for the office to have jurisdiction, a local law enforcement agency somewhere in the state of Ohio would have to open an investigation and then request their assistance.

Toward the conclusion of the report, the ODE lists each of its recommendations once more and explicitly explains how there are virtually no possible solutions to solve any of the problems presented by Bishop Sycamore. "Can action be taken to prevent Bishop Sycamore from continuing to operate?" the report asks.

That answer is no, because the ODE has no authority to prohibit them from operating. Could legal action be a reasonable method? The report indicates that previous legal cases set a precedent that "an attendance officer or a local board of education cannot obtain a court order to prevent a school from operating merely because the school does not meet the minimum standards. Instead, the Court believed a proper remedy was to prosecute the parents for sending their children to such a school." On a legal basis, parents would be held responsible, not the school. To the ODE, that was not a good solution. "Based on the Court's holding, it appears that for a court order to issue, a litigant would have to prove actionable injury to the health, morals, or safety of a person. Without such a showing, a way to keep children from attending a non-chartered, non-tax-supported school that fails to meet the minimum standards is, cruelly, to prosecute their parents."

"Why was Bishop Sycamore High School allowed to operate?" the report asks rhetorically. The answer to that question is perhaps the most damning indication of the department's inability to act. "To answer this question, the question's premise must be rejected. Ohio law does not provide the Department with any authority to allow such schools to operate or disallow the operation of those that violate the law. Bishop Sycamore

High School submitted the paperwork required by rule. The rule does not provide the Department with the authority to review and approve, or disapprove, a form or a school's operation." The report's only advice is that the ODE should review its internal procedures and "ensure they address when and how to escalate concerns" expressed by people involved.

Currently, there are no active criminal investigations into Bishop Sycamore or its founders in relation to the school. The changes to ODE policies the Department would like to see would have to come from the Ohio legislature. No new laws have been passed to prevent this behavior in the future. In fact, none have even been introduced for consideration. And between the largely performative report and the lack of repercussions, Johnson feels vindicated and "harassed" for no reason.

"I didn't create the rules. I didn't even find the loopholes. I just followed the loopholes that everyone else was using," he said, claiming the ODE investigation was "bullshit." Emboldened by the report, he took specific note of the ODE's inability to punish him or anyone else involved in Bishop Sycamore.

"They can say whatever they want about what they do or don't like, but at the end of it, unless the laws change, there's nothing they can do to keep Bishop Sycamore from functioning as a school. We didn't do anything illegal. [The report is] just people yelling about stuff. Why do you think the governor said, 'We're going to have to find a way for these kids to graduate' and all that? You guys had them in four years of fucked up schools before they even got to us. So you obviously don't think that much about education, otherwise you'd care about the fact these kids came to us with a 1.2 GPA. How the hell are you letting kids graduate with a 1.2?"

Johnson neglects to mention the fact that not every person involved with Bishop Sycamore had already graduated high school. At least three students were minors who did not have a high school diploma. While those children were in their care, Johnson, Peterson, and Bishop Sycamore did nothing to ensure that any of the minors or adults enrolled in their program actually improved their GPA or focused on school in any way. The students who did receive any education did it in spite of the program, not because of it. Bishop Sycamore partnered with Graduation Alliance to create an online curriculum for its students in August of 2020. Services began in October of 2020.

According to the ODE report, "Graduation Alliance informed Department staff that Bishop Sycamore High School initially enrolled 19 students. The students' ages ranged from 15 to 20. The credits remaining toward graduation at the time of students' enrollment ranged from zero to 20. Many of the school's students were in the online program for partial months. One student enrolled for one day. By late January 2021, only five students remained enrolled. The relationship between Graduation Alliance and Bishop Sycamore deteriorated after Bishop Sycamore fell behind on the agreed upon payment plan of $239 per month (which was prorated by the number of days students were enrolled in the month) for Graduation Alliance's services. Despite Bishop Sycamore's nonpayment of service fees, Graduation Alliance continued to provide online access to the school's students. Upon termination of its relationship with Bishop Sycamore, Graduation Alliance offered full scholarships for the five students who remained in the program. Four students accepted the scholarships. The fifth student enrolled in a public district."

Johnson's claim that the State of Ohio doesn't "think that much about education," is up for debate, but one thing is certain: No one thought less about education than Bishop Sycamore.

So after a nationally televised embarrassment and a months-long State of Ohio investigation, what is to prevent a Bishop Sycamore situation from happening again? Currently, nothing. Ohio has not updated its policies and identified weaknesses to prevent bad actors from exploiting the system again—and Johnson certainly will.

It was more than a year after the ESPN game when Johnson tweeted, "We are coming back next year."

15

THE RIGHTS OF KIDS

In September of 1990, the United Nations Committee on the Rights of the Child oversaw the adoption of an international treaty called the Convention on the Rights of the Child. On its surface, the document seemed like an obvious point of agreement for the developed world. It aimed to protect the rights of children worldwide, defining a child as any human being under the age of 18. The CRC calls for United Nations members to ensure the protection of a child's right to a name and nationality, freedom of speech and thought, access to health care and education, freedom from torture, abuse, and exploitation, as well as banning capital punishment. The treaty drew nearly unanimous support from UN member states. Even today, UNICEF says the CRC "has helped transform children's lives around the world."

In 1990, all but two UN member states ratified the treaty. Nearly 25 years later, one of those outliers, Somalia, ratified the treaty with a later UN addition and CRC holdout, South Sudan, soon to follow. That leaves just one country who has yet to ratify: the United States of America.

The country's United Nations policies don't dictate American sports legislation, but they do match the nation's attitude toward legislation aimed at protecting our children. In his work at The School District of Philadelphia, Dr. James Patrick Lynch has been a loud proponent of reform for governance of youth athletics. From his perspective, the "lack of consistency or standards" on a nationwide scale leaves American students open to the possibility of exploitation. "We have 51 state athletic associations and each one has their own constitution and bylaws just like each of our states have their own laws and legislations," he said. "So to a certain extent, that's ripe for this kind of abuse."

Nearly three decades after the UN's adoption of the CRC, Tom Farrey was traveling abroad to learn more about how European organizations run youth sports programs. "I wouldn't say school sports are broken; it's not a broken model," he said. "But it's a model that isn't always clear about why it exists and what the purpose of school-based sports is, and that's in part because school sports are treated as extracurricular, not core to the educational mission or academic enterprise. It's coached by people who are not teachers and who are not adopted into the larger purpose of the school. They interpret their role as aggregating and driving talent to win games on Friday nights, and that's where it kind of separates from the larger purpose of school sports."

He was searching for ways that United States sports can emulate and learn from various European models, and found himself studying the way that Norway—a nation of just about 5 million people—could be so effective in the Olympic games.

Along the way, he discovered that Norway—inspired by the CRC—had created a document called Children's Rights in Sport. Adopted in 2007, the legislation sets boundaries and guidelines for youth participation in athletics. The very first sentence in the document highlights the difference in attitudes between Scandinavian and American sporting cultures: "Children are engaged in sports because they enjoy it. Together with their friends they have experiences and learn lessons that will last them a lifetime. This is the foundation that all coaches, managers, and parents must safeguard and develop further." Children's Rights in Sport outlines the importance of non-discriminatory practices, safety, fostering friendships among players, allowing children to choose their sports, and a variety of other practices aimed at creating a more healthy athletic dynamic.

Through his travels and research, Farrey found that Norway wasn't alone. A variety of other nations had similar legislation, which led him to the discovery of the CRC and the realization that the United States was drastically lagging behind other developed nations in the area of childhood sporting protections. "A key was building a better base of the sports system," he said. "Central to that was identifying and being very clear on what the rights of children are. The bottom line is that the rights of kids have not been defined in this country. So I thought, 'Let's just do it anyway, from a non-government point of view.'"

Back in the States, Farrey and his team built a group that set out to create a similar document, regardless of whether it would carry any weight. The idea, he said, was to put *something* on paper that gave guidance to those who may be putting systems in place for kids in athletics. In addition to Aspen Institute staff, the committee creating the document included representatives from Athletes for Hope, the University of Baltimore's Center for Sport and the Law, the Centre for Sport & Human Rights, the Power of Sport Lab, the U.S. Center for Safesport, and more. When it was finished, their document earned support from more than 60 nationwide organizations, including the U.S. Olympic & Paralympic Committee, YMCA, National Recreation and Park Association, Little League International, ESPN, and many more, as well as more than 250 members of the Athletes for Hope network.

The committee's final Children's Bill of Rights in Sports identifies eight rights:

1) **To play sports**: Organizations should make every effort to accommodate children's interests to participate, and to help them play with peers from diverse backgrounds.

2) **To safe and healthy environments**: Children have the right to play in settings free from all forms of abuse (physical, emotional, sexual), hazing, violence, and neglect.
3) **To qualified program leaders**: Children have the right to play under the care of coaches and other adults who pass background checks and are trained in key competencies.
4) **To developmentally appropriate play**: Children have a right to play at a level commensurate with their physical, mental, and emotional maturity, and their emerging athletic ability. They should be treated as young people first, athletes second.
5) **To share in the planning and delivery of their activities**: Children have the right to share their viewpoints with coaches and for their insights to be incorporated into activities.
6) **To an equal opportunity for personal growth**: Programs should invest equally in all child athletes, free of discrimination based on any personal or family characteristic.
7) **To be treated with dignity**: Children have the right to participate in environments that promote the values of sportsmanship, of respect for opponents, officials, and the game.
8) **To enjoy themselves**: Children have the right to participate in activities they consider fun, and which foster the development of friendships and social bonds.

Measured against the standards of Bishop Sycamore, it's easy to see how American sports institutions could benefit from an all-encompassing bill of rights or similar document.

Bishop Sycamore did indeed aim "to play sports," but their goals had nothing to do with accommodating children's interests or helping play with peers from diverse backgrounds. Rather than emphasizing "safe and healthy environments," Johnson and his team scraped together living situations in whatever way they could, which put them in danger of nearly all the warnings listed above. At no point was Bishop Sycamore led by "qualified program leaders," and there was no training "in key competencies" or clear standards for a background check. No consideration was given to "developmentally appropriate play," and the use of students who were older—sometimes significantly—than the competition shows how little attention was paid to that concept. It was largely impossible for the Bishop Sycamore students to "share in the planning and delivery of their activities" because that planning was nearly always a combination of slapdash, last minute, or not planned at all. By definition, there was no attempt to "invest equally in all child athletes" because the school was tailored to those who could potentially earn a college scholarship. Only the kids themselves could say whether they were treated with "dignity," though the many tales of neglect and fraudulent behavior seem to make that impossible. And while there were certainly accounts of players enjoying themselves, the "development of friendships and social bonds" was never an emphasis.

Farrey is proud of what the team came up with, but he sees it as a very simple stance. "None of it is rocket science," he said with a laugh. Unfortunately, turning the document into a model for legislation that has teeth and can help dictate actual, meaningful punishment for those who don't abide by the rules is another issue. "There's great demand to treat kids better than we're treating them right now, but organizations are not being held accountable to that demand."

* * *

At the basis of America's unique relationship with our amateur athletics is our connection between sports and education. As early as grade school, sports are intrinsically connected to school—if they're available at all. Travel teams begin popping up before middle school, and tryouts are more discussed than the healthy exercise that athletics were meant to facilitate. So for Tyrre Burks and other athletic reformers, returning to the baseline of non-competitive play—especially in low-income neighborhoods—is critical.

"In elementary schools in a lot of these neighborhoods, sports programs don't exist anymore," he said. "You either have to pay for sports or you have to be really talented. It used to be that you could be a part of recreational sports and you could just play. Now, 80 percent of youth sports is competitive.

You try out and you pay. The problem is the way the United States has created the motivator for getting to the next level. No other country has that same motivator because they don't have the same system that creates the bad things that happen in youth, college, and pro sports."

"For the 39 percent of kids who play interscholastic sports in this country, it is primarily education-based activity," Farrey said. "It's really just that top 5 percent and especially that top 1 percent of the best that gets all the attention and represents most of the problems."

Farrey suggests that schools are simply asking the wrong questions as they think about athletics. Rather than trying to assess the best athletes at a school and attempting to put them together to form a team of 10-year-olds that can win a championship, he believes the system could be upended and streamlined by taking a different approach: trying to understand the *type* of sports interest each student has. For instance, some students might be looking for friendly competition. Other students might be looking for a way to exercise. And, of course, there will be those who want to develop their skills in order to play in college or even professionally. The goal, in all of those instances, would be to create opportunities for students of all levels to play, whether in a school-sanctioned team or with a local club, and ensure that the model is not exploitative or exclusionary. "The point should be to start with the health needs of the entire student body and then design from there," he said, "as opposed to creating teams in all the same sports that have been around for 50 years and then sports in school becomes about the very best athletes."

Lynch sees this dynamic as the natural state of competition and something that all competitors naturally understand. For him, the best example of the ideal situation is the college environment, where the vast majority of students play because they want to stay fit or exercise with friends, while schools still make highly competitive programs available for the elite athletes among them. "Colleges engage so many of their kids just through recreation, whether it's yoga classes or soccer teams or three-on-three basketball tournaments. These are kids who will never touch a basketball for the St. Joe's men's basketball team, but want to have some fun and have a beer afterward."

But the solution isn't as simple as legislating away those problems—at least in the form of statewide athletic associations. Similar to OHSAA, Ohio's regulatory body that tried to raise red flags about Bishop Sycamore, organizations across the country exist mainly as organizers and event planners. They do things like host state championship tournaments and gather teams into divisions. But, as the Bishop Sycamore saga informs, they're often toothless in the face of blatant disregard for their rules. Lynch has seen that many times, and has even found that the very existence of those organizations can be a challenge. By putting rules and restrictions in place, those organizations necessitate a more focused approach to school sports. By requiring schools, coaches, players, parents, and anyone else involved to act a certain way and go through certain procedures, governing bodies are effectively *mandating* that youth sports are treated like the minor leagues rather than friendly competition.

"These high school athletic associations come in and regulate. They say, 'You can't have a team at your school that isn't regulated by the state association,' and that brings in all the extra standards and restrictions," Lynch said. "We're talking about kids who just want to kick a ball around or shoot some hoops twice a week.... They're not playing in the state championship, but they very well could associate that 'open gym' with a positive experience, which could make them come to school more and better their attendance rate. You can't teach kids if they don't come through the door, so how can we incentivize kids to go to school every day?"

Fortunately, unlike many conversations about widespread reform, there are plenty of alternative athletics models from which to draw inspiration. In Europe, where soccer reigns supreme but basketball, rugby, cricket, and other sports still have a professional pathway, the club system dominates the landscape. Rather than intertwining school and sports, professional teams begin working with players at an extremely young age. The famed academy of sporting titans FC Barcelona, known as La Masia, takes recruits between six and 11 years old. Children are accepted into these programs because of their sporting abilities and become full-time students with an education curated by the program. Because all students are there for the same reason, double standards are eliminated and goals are clear. And by separating these organizations—which are open and honest about their desire to make money off of the sport—from school institutions that want to offer athletics as part of a program for student health, the purpose and goal of each is more clearly aligned. Of course European systems have their own flaws, but Farrey, Lynch, and Burks all agree that American athletics could take some cues from our European counterparts.

"If you have talent at age 16 or 14, you have value to certain organizations who can monetize it, and that's not going away," Farrey said. "We're not going to put that genie back in the bottle. So the question is, what do you do for that 5 percent of kids who are really chasing downstream financial opportunities, including college athletic scholarships? How do we treat that piece of the puzzle? In Europe, if you have talent like that in basketball or other sports, you may have a professional contract starting at age 16. You may be working with affiliated organizations and being groomed by a club like FC Barcelona as early as 14. You look at players who have come to the NBA from Europe ... and if you're truly in that 1 percent, there's no overlap whatsoever with the school environment. You get your training, you're monetized, and you're compensated through a sports structure."

"I don't think that's a terrible thing. In fact, I would like to see the NBA, for example, take control of its pipeline. Make a U-14 team. Have a club in every NBA or G League city. There's a small group of players who are still being required to go to school while being groomed for a sport structure that has some standards around it and a clear purpose as to why that exists. We see this in Europe, and it's not a problem. It's not a terrible thing to put a highly talented athlete into a professional sport system as early as 14 or 16. I would like to see that piece of it removed from [American] high schools."

* * *

America's newest and biggest issue in high school athletics is the new wave of laws allowing for the monetization of amateur athletes' name, image, and likeness. While he doesn't see it as an inherently bad or impossible-to-implement idea, the problem comes in adoption. "Some states are allowing it, some are not, and it's going to create massive inequity across the country," he said. "And in 99 percent of the states that do allow it, the schools cannot be privy or part of those negotiations. So it's like the wild, wild west, and that's only going to make the landscape worse for abuse. We've already seen it at the college level. Each state having their different bylaws does kind of allow something like [Bishop Sycamore] to happen. States talk to each other to some extent, but it's not like they are investigating every single school across the country."

For Burks, who can reflect on his own journey through amateur and into professional sports in addition to watching his son navigate the process today, the blurring lines between amateur and professional sports create a problem that's "only getting worse." His fear, he said, is that the get-rich-quick dream of a gigantic NIL deal can make kids less motivated by sports, academics, or a drive to succeed and more motivated by a paycheck that seems like it's in reach.

"Sixteen-year-olds can now make money on their name and license, and you've added more pressure to be successful in sports at a younger age. There's even more pressure on these kids now, not to go to college anymore, but to be known and to build a brand by being good at sports at that age. Now, I don't need to go pro, I just need to be a really, really good high school basketball player, have a huge following, have college teams looking at me, and suddenly I've got an NIL deal. I can be the next Zion Williamson, with a million followers on Instagram at 17. If I can do that, I can probably retire."

What if a kid with no fallback plan puts all their eggs into that basket? "What happens most of the time is a sad story."

Lynch is adamant that federal guidelines are "very necessary" in order to clean up the environment of youth sports across the country. He's hopeful that the NIL issue—which involves large amounts of money, a key factor in forcing decisions—will spur change, but sees federal regulations as a much more important step for legislating access, opportunity, and a less exploitative environment for kids in sports. And without those laws, the gaps and inequities that exist in our society at large will continue to affect sports, while those interested in exploiting children or taking advantage of the world of amateur sports will continue to benefit. "What we see as a lot of barriers and structure deficiencies that are out of our control because it's under the state guidance is very different from what you'd see a mile down the road in the suburbs with kids who have been playing since they were in diapers."

As is often the case in attempting legislative reform, the problem with creating or implementing changes to America's sports structure comes down to a question of who benefits from that change. Take the football pipeline as the most simple example. The NFL is the top of the American football pyramid. That organization is currently operating without a youth or academy league, saving a massive cost when compared to European sports clubs. The reason they don't have to pay for that system is because of college football, where universities and the NCAA foot the bill for infrastructure that creates talent that will eventually move on to the NFL. The reason they foot that bill is because college football makes up a behemoth of an industry, generating more than $1 billion in revenue each year. In turn, that funding helps fund other sports, academic programs, and more. But the NCAA doesn't pay for its development either, thanks to high schools operating under a very similar model. High-performing high school programs become marketing entities unto themselves, and private schools can charge extremely high fees to bring students to a school where they have a greater chance of progressing on to the next level. Each step of the way, player talents are being used to generate revenue. And each step of the way, that money trumps the desire for reform.

"They're only going to wake up to the problem if they see some self-interest in doing so," Farrey said. "If they perceive that there's less talent coming through the pipeline that could sell their product later on, they might act. But I'm not sure they believe that. They might act if they have a legal or liability concern—concussions could be interesting there. Could you be held accountable for promoting activity that is to the detriment of the health of youth? If governments or insurance companies hold the powers that be accountable for that, you might see them act. But in the absence of any financial incentive or penalty to act, you're probably not going to see them do so. Then who becomes the catalyst?"

Curt Caffey, who is in the trenches of the world of high school athletics in his role as athletic director of Patriot Preparatory Academy in Columbus, says there needs to be some kind of organization with the power to validate—or not—a school's status. Without them, he sees more room for corruption and the endangering of player safety. "Otherwise, it's just going to continue to expand and expand and expand. At some point, somebody has got to put the brakes on this kind of stuff happening, because in our world, out there on the street, there's a lot of players who play on the kids and the parents. That's their whole drive. But I think there's an avenue [to create] a governing body that could be put in place specifically for this sector of athletics.... I think they should create a checklist of validity for these organizations. I think that's the biggest problem—not validating what's being presented, not just letting it go because Coach Johnny said, 'We're okay.' Let's validate that you're okay, and I think that could be the work of a [governing] body."

Lynch doesn't believe we're capable of getting away from the ties that bind sports to education, and he's not entirely sure that's a bad thing. "We're not going to drive into Texas and tell people they don't have Friday night lights anymore," he said with a laugh. "But I think it's just something to be aware of so that as we try to move the needle and reverse the trends that have gotten us into a state where you see Bishop Sycamores rise up, we need to be understanding and cognizant of that. We're not going to reverse the school sports, but how do we ensure that the community sports provide recreation focus and access for all? I think we need to keep the great things that school sports offer—teamwork, camaraderie, relationship building, mental and physical wellness, and health—but I think the reform is key. We need to look at how we expand the high school sports model to include everybody."

Not everyone is so optimistic, however. For Burks, the NIL shift simply represents the next evolution of a money-based system, and one that only moves in one direction. "We'll never go back," he said. "The pendulum has swung, and it's not coming back. We're in it, and money is being made. Youth sports is a $20 billion industry. More money is going in and more professionalism, structure, and pressure is going in to create more demand for more revenue. That's the American way."

16

TOTALLY EVIL, MALEVOLENT PEOPLE

Back in 2018, when COF Academy still existed, Roy Johnson had yet to be questioned by the Secret Service, and Bishop Sycamore hadn't even been dreamed up, Arthur Harmon was adamant: there was zero connection between the American Methodist Episcopal Third District and Johnson, Jay Richardson, or the Richard Allen Group. The Third District's attorney, who represented the church publicly and in legal matters, was unwilling to talk about the matter at any further length because there was simply nothing to discuss. But after four long years and a string of legal cases, and in the wake of Bishop Sycamore becoming a nationally recognized scandal, Harmon had apparently taken some time to reflect.

"I just think that everything points down to Reverend Thompson."

As it turns out, Harmon had been aware of Johnson and Richardson for years before COF Academy ever launched. In an interview in late 2022, he admitted that he remembers the pair, as the Richard Allen Group, presenting economic development ideas to the church even before their insurance plans began.

"Now with the Richard Allen Group, they had some grandiose thoughts about how the church could benefit in certain ways from some of these, I call them schemes, and plans that they had," he said. "The church, a lot of times, does listen to these groups that come in. In this case, I'll admit that the Richard Allen Group had some plans that were very unique, I would say, as to how the church could benefit from certain things. They had insurance, that was one of them. Another one was real estate obligations that would help the community and benefit the church and that kind of thing. Very interesting. I even found it to be interesting myself."

But unlike Johnson's depiction of those presentations, Harmon made it clear that not only had the Richard Allen Group never been formally partnered with the church, it would have had to clear a number of hurdles before that could have been possible thanks to a byzantine method of governance among member churches and the factions of which they belong. The AME Church is divided into episcopal districts—of which the Columbus chapter is the third. Those districts serve as the administrations of the annual conference between the districts. Each annual conference is the individual church's, and the governance of each of the annual conferences is with the trustees of the annual conference. The episcopal district itself is subject to the authority of the annual conferences. According to Harmon, at the annual conferences and other periodic meetings, members gather to take care of legislative business and other matters. At those meetings, groups also give presentations of ideas that they believe would benefit the church or its members. Often, those presentations deal with fiscal plans, advice, or other proposed changes, usually related to fundraising or improved communication and contact among members. Insurance was not an uncommon topic to have presented at these get-togethers. But when people would present an idea at these conferences, a passing mention of approval or an affirmation of the plan wasn't a binding agreement or a formal adoption. And that, in Harmon's estimation, is where any of Johnson's plans involving the church started and stopped.

"The allegations that Roy Johnson and his group made is that they made agreements—these were the allegations—with the Bishop," Harmon said. "First off, the Bishop doesn't have the authority to make any types of decisions as they were alleging. Second of all, any type of action such as that would had to have been taken to each of the annual conferences to be approved by them. None of that ever happened.... The best I could see as to what happened is they made a presentation. One of [them] was there would be a real estate angle whereby, somehow, the church would benefit from the sale of real estate to its members. Its members would get a break or consideration for the purchase of property, homes, and a result of the commission or whatever from the sale that the church could benefit and then the Richard Allen group could obviously benefit. What they wanted the church to do was to encourage their members to engage. If they were going to buy a house, buy it from the Richard Allen Group and the church would then get a percentage of that, was the plan."

Harmon said Bishop McKinley Young, who died in January of 2019, "never agreed to that plan." He referenced the ongoing legal battles, in which a magistrate proved that a formal connection between the Richard Allen Group and the AME Third District never existed, and said there was "no quid pro quo or anything" else in place. Even if Young had approved the plan, Harmon said, he would have had to take the issue back to the broader AME Church leadership that governs the entire nationwide organization. And when it comes to a school or a football team, Harmon is absolutely sure AME Church leadership would never have gone for it. That's because the church already has its hands full running two programs that it can barely keep afloat.

In addition to its member churches and the organizations within them, the AME Church operates two affiliated schools in the Dayton, Ohio, area: Wilberforce University and Payne Theological Seminary. Both are located in Wilberforce, near Dayton suburb Xenia. In Harmon's telling, the two schools are "always struggling to survive," and require a lot of funds from the broader church in order to stay operational. "So when Roy Johnson and Jay and them wanted to start some school and have, according to them, the Third District finance it, the Third District had no ability to do that, and barely are keeping the schools that we have afloat. It just doesn't make sense when you look at it as to the church being a part of this scheme." But, he said, their ideas did draw *some* interest.

"There was a treasurer of the Third District who may have been, I guess, listening more closely to that plan than anybody else and was basically, I think, encouraging the church to go down that road. But the church never did go down that road." That treasurer was Rev. Taylor Thompson, a longtime AME Church minister and administrator who has, since 2019, relocated to Canton, Ohio, where he serves as a pastor. Johnson and others have plenty of examples of Rev. Thompson taking part in conversations about the Richard Allen Group, and a variety of people saw him at events and even financial discussions about finances related to COF Academy. His signature could even be found on the $100,000 check that found its way into an account under the Richard Allen Group's name operated by Johnson. Rev. Thompson, however, had completely denied any involvement with the Richard Allen Group in 2019. But, to Harmon, that feels unlikely.

"There was one thing I could not figure out: somehow, $100,000 from the church was deposited into an account for the Richard Allen group," he said. "I try not to indict anybody, but I believe that Rev. Thompson was more involved in this than he admits. He was pushing this thing and may have even, I can't say [for sure], but it seems like it's very possible that he even tried to convince Roy and Jay that, being the treasurer of the church—and of course the treasurer has no power to promise any of these things—that the church would support them. He was definitely involved in the insurance scheme, I do know that. I was commissioned by the Bishop—Bishop Young, who died shortly after that—to look into this and find out what was going on. The best I could figure out, if there was any connection to the church, it was an unauthorized connection that involved Rev. Thompson. I think Rev. Thompson got taken in thinking, 'Here are some schemes whereby the church—the Episcopal District and the individual churches—could receive a profit.' And if he was able to bring that home, then he would get a lot of accolades from the church."

To Harmon, it would make sense for Rev. Thompson to want to find a financial boost for the church. Many of the AME Church's buildings have been around for decades or longer, and upkeep on facilities like those can be an expensive proposition. With church membership dwindling all across the country, AME Church funds have become harder to come by, and Harmon admitted that delivering a clever plan to find some funding would be "a big feather in somebody's cap." And while he can't prove the involvement of Rev. Thompson—who has never replied to requests for comment since abruptly hanging up the phone in 2019—he can't help but feel that Johnson and Richardson aren't actually corrupt enough to have been lying completely about their contact with church officials. "If I assume that Roy Johnson and Jay weren't just totally evil, malevolent people, I would have to assume that they thought that they were into the structure of the Third District, whereby the Third District was going to support them in what they did. And if they thought that—and I talked to Bishop Young, who denied it of course—but I just think that everything points down to Rev. Thompson. Everything seems to point down to him. He never did admit it."

As for Johnson's brief and intimidating brush with the Secret Service? Harmon is pretty sure Rev. Thompson was behind that, too. "He even turned against Roy and Jay by calling the federals, the FBI and all that, saying that somehow the check was misdirected from going into the church's account. [Rev. Thompson said] the $100,000 check somehow got into the account for the Richard Allen Group, and that he was told by the bank representative that it was supposed to go into a church fund and it actually went into the account for the Richard Allen Group. So he denies it every day and all that, but I kinda think he had a little more to do with that."

But even with all those factors at play, in Harmon's eyes, Johnson—in particular—and Richardson aren't off the hook. "Roy, I think, was the mastermind of it. He did some really fraudulent things. You've seen the court filings and decisions and things like that; they did a lot of things. There are at least a couple court cases—the one I was directly involved in, then another, both with banks—where they had gotten $100,000 from each bank indicating that they were the actual secretary and treasurer and in charge of the Third District of the AME Church, which is just crazy. The banks were fooled. Well, the one bank got their money back."

Harmon says the insurance scheme that Johnson presented wasn't as philanthropic and above board as Johnson claimed it was. Rather than simply being upfront about the way the policies would work, Harmon said Johnson was telling church members in 2013 that if they signed up for the policies he was offering, their premiums would be paid through a grant, which meant that the members wouldn't have to pay for the policies that would eventually be paid out to the church. The grant didn't exist. In other words, Johnson was telling people that they could donate a lasting legacy to the church in their name—for free.

Harmon said RAG tried a second insurance scheme again around 2016. This time, they framed the policies so that the AME Third District acted as the employer, offering employee policies through a corporate group life insurance method. But that plan was ill-fated from the start, because the AME Church only listed about five employees at the time, so when everything was put on paper, the church had around 100 employees insured in spite of only employing five. The result of both schemes was the cancellation of the pair's insurance licenses, which Harmon himself helped to facilitate, along with informing the insurance company they had been working with. "I talked to the Department of Insurance and informed them of this, and they were very highly upset because they said, 'We canceled their licenses already.'… As soon as I talked to the insurance company, they backed out of it. They didn't know that was the actual situation."

Ultimately, Harmon struggles to get past the fact that Johnson did "some really fraudulent things." But, as he estimates, he isn't the "completely evil" person that would be required for him to have fabricated his entire story. And in another world, Harmon even thinks COF Academy could have come to fruition. "I'll be truthful, I think the scheme that Roy had put together in some situations could've worked! It could've worked, but they did need somebody to bankroll the thing. The AME Church, or the Third District, was not that type of entity, did not have the power to do that, [and they] didn't get the approval from the general conference or from their own annual conference. That kind of shows that there really was no substance to it."

17

AM I 100 PERCENT INNOCENT IN THIS?

Roy Johnson loves the 1965 song "Don't Let Me Be Misunderstood" by The Animals. He says he likes to "constantly refer to and listen to" the song, and feels a connection with its lyrics. He often knows why people are upset with him, but often feels that he hasn't done anything to deserve their wrath.

Baby, can you understand me now?
Sometimes I get a little mad
Don't you know, no one alive can always be an angel
When things go wrong, I seem to go bad
I'm just a soul whose intentions are good
Oh Lord, please don't let me be misunderstood

One day, at a court-mandated appointment, Roy Johnson's therapist told him that he's willing to hurt himself in order to help others. He's not sure whether that's true or not, but he takes the professional's word for it. "He's a therapist, so just based on him talking to people about me and about things that I've done, he said I have a vigilante problem. I see an issue and I'm like, 'Oh, this isn't right so

I'm going to do my best to fix it even if it ends up affecting myself.'"

Johnson has been going to therapy for two years. It was originally mandated as part of his domestic violence charge, but he said he's no longer required to go. Instead, he's still visiting the therapist because he "thought it was beneficial in other areas of my life." But Johnson doesn't think he *needs* therapy. And he doesn't think his therapist thinks so either. "I go to therapy for anger management, and he's like, 'I understand why they sent you here because that's how the system works, but you don't really fit the bill for anger management issues. You're 40 years old, you've never been arrested, you've never had any fights or anything.'"

In the wake of his debut on national television and the chaos that followed, Johnson has been feeling introspective. Along the way, his interviews with HBO have given him questions to ponder. For instance: Is he a liar?

It's complicated.

"HBO said to me, 'You realize there are a lot of things that are going to be said that you won't like,' and I said, 'Well, as long as it's the truth, there's nothing for me to not like.' And he said, 'Well, you identified yourself as being a liar.' Of course, because I'm not stupid enough to sit up here and be like, 'I'm not a liar.' I'm in a catch-22. I have to be a liar. Because people will say I said things to them that didn't come through. Was I lying to them? Was I selling them? I'm [like] a used car salesman. Am I a scam artist? There's a lot of gray area. If it's true, it's true. If it's not, it's not. The very fact that I live in the gray area and now you're asking me not to live in the gray area is going to be a problem.... I get pissed off when people lie, but I lie to people. How can I justify that? I can't. That's the yin and yang. That's being human; that's part of it. How many people cheat on their spouses but don't want their spouses cheating on them? Isn't that hypocritical? Yes. It's a hypocritical world. I'm a hypocritical person."

In spite of everything, the people whose lives are permanently affected by Johnson's decisions and lies—whether those lies came in a gray area or not—somehow share the same complicated stance on Johnson's character.

"Something keeps him going. Right or wrong, good intentions or not, he's brilliant," said Deryck Richardson, who reached out to Johnson in the months following the IMG Academy game. The two hadn't spoken in years, but he felt compelled to check in, sending a text that said, "Hey man, I hope your mental health is okay." Deryck still sees Johnson as "a genuine guy," and has a difficult time reconciling what he witnessed. "My wife asked me, 'Do you still believe the church screwed Roy?' She said, 'Are you sure you guys weren't just being played by Roy the entire time?' But that's impossible. I was at the church when our assistant was with the Bishop. The Bishop was [there]. It would be impossible that he masterminded this whole plan to screw us. I still believe that money was coming, money never came and Roy scrambled. He got it done how he could get it done."

Ulysses Hall has as much reason to hate Roy Johnson as anyone involved in COF Academy or Bishop Sycamore. Hall said he "gained a ton of weight" because of the stress of the situation, and spent so much of his own money while not getting paid that he's still recovering financially. At one point, Johnson gave Hall the keys to a storage locker that he said the church would be paying for. When Hall quit the program, he arrived to find the storage locker cleaned out. "I lost clothes, memorabilia—not just football stuff, personal items. My little brother passed in 1999 and I had photos, pictures of my family, very personal items, TVs, golf clubs. I've never recouped any of that stuff." He estimates he lost nearly $20,000 worth of personal items—some priceless.

Hall wishes he had listened to his mom and grandmother, who told him, "Don't trust this guy," and a girlfriend who told him, "Roy is a con man; he's a swindler." But ultimately, Hall is hesitant to blame Roy for everything. To him, it still comes back to the AME Church. "I think early on he had good intentions, and I believe it was all real because I was at the meetings. I don't know the dealings that went on between he and the church, but you don't plan a multimillion dollar project like that and then all of the sudden just back out. Something happened where they said, 'Uh-uh, we're not doing this.' I want to know, from the AME church, when the kids were already there, why didn't you guys put up the funding to see it through? And if it wasn't going to work after a year, you just have to eat that funding. But you don't just leave me and other people hanging out with a bunch of kids. Y'all just left us hanging, and I still have that gripe."

Talk of Johnson being a "con man" reminds filmmaker Martin Desmond Roe of one of his favorite quotes from Johnson during the filming of Roe's HBO documentary on Bishop Sycamore. "He said, 'Well, you know there's that TV show, *Black-ish*? I don't know if I'm a con man, but I'm a con man-ish.'" And like almost everyone else, Roe has a challenging time reconciling his feelings toward Johnson.

"If you go all the way back, he targeted old people with insurance and he targeted kids with sports dreams. He's a classic confidence man, a classic trickster. And yet, he does bring some sparkle to the world. A lot of kids got hurt. The film really focuses on the impact on those kids. Kids got hurt physically, they got hurt emotionally, they got hurt logistically—[quarterback] Trillian [Harris] lost *another* year because of Roy. It's hard to forgive those things.... I don't see him as evil. I think he's deeply misguided and deeply narcissistic. I think he's truly apathetic to other people in a way that is mind-blowing. But he dances through the raindrops with a grace that is hard to not credit with some value."

In one of his interviews with HBO, Johnson was asked for three words to describe himself. He chose insecure, liar, and smart. He says he's charismatic *because* of his insecurities, and recognizes his own deep desire for people to like him. He even shows glimpses of acknowledging the problems he's caused. "I made a mistake; I'm willing to take that on." But he's also confident in his status as the main character of his own story. Asked whether he's the hero or the villain of that story, he's unsure. "That depends on what you would consider Robin Hood—is Robin Hood a good guy or a bad guy? Robin Hood has a lot more hero in him than I do, but I think I have a lot of altruism in my actions. It's hard to say."

However, that altruism doesn't extend to the players who spoke about the hardships they faced because of Johnson or during his care. For instance, the three New York–based players who spoke to the *New York Times* are, in Johnson's estimation, just complaining about problems that are unrelated to him. He blames those students, and others, for not taking the right approach to school, football, and life. And in a glimpse of his more combative side, he said he sometimes daydreams about getting those players and others together for a "reunion episode" like they have at the end of reality television shows.

"I would love to sit down and talk to them and say, 'I want to hear all your gripes. What are your problems? And now, when you're done with your problems, I'm going to show you why they're not a problem.' I want to start this off saying, 'Did you know how this started? Did you know the church brought you out here and then turned around and basically said fuck off?' Instead of me walking away and doing to you what people normally do, I tried to keep it going. Is that right or wrong? It all comes down to perspective."

At the heart of any assessment of Johnson is that tension between his charisma and ability to self-reflect along with his combative nature and consistent willingness to ignore the problems of others. Most people who have spent any time around the man find these attributes difficult to square.

"I cannot help but like Roy," Roe said. "I cannot help but find, in him, this inner child and his desperate desire to be loved and to sparkle and to matter and to do things. It's so present and it's so charming, and I can't help but feel that if he just had a passion in his life that didn't involve children, that so much more leeway would be granted to him. But so much extraordinary leeway *has* been granted to him.... A saving grace of the Roy Johnson story, and the reason we don't find him evil, is because of his own incompetence. If Roy had actually made any money off of this, he would just be a villain. But because he didn't, because he got busted before he made anything, he can try and dress himself up in this do-gooder armor. But it's completely hollow; it doesn't ring true."

That assessment is one that Johnson can agree with. At the end of every road, for him, is the church's stonewalling of what he believes could have been and still could be a great and impactful project. For him, the people and organizations hurt along the way pale in comparison to the injustice that was imparted on him. "If you can't see how the church is responsible for all this, then I don't care to hear about some dumb shit about I didn't pay for a fucking bus. In the grand scheme of things, that's not the problem. It's not."

"On a scale of one to 10—10 being I'm the most evil person in the world, zero being I'm an angel—I'm probably a seven," he said with uproarious laughter. "I got a lot of work to do. But that's how I feel about it. Am I 100 percent innocent in this? Absolutely not." The Animals would agree.

Oh, now don't you know I'm human
I got my faults just like anyone
And sometimes I find myself, alone, regretting
Some foolish thing, some sinful thing I've done
I'm just a soul whose intentions are good
Oh Lord, please don't let me be misunderstood

Johnson and Jay Richardson no longer have a business relationship, but Johnson believes the pair are still friends, and says they feel similarly about the four-year ordeal. "He thinks everything that everyone on my side thinks: the church caused this whole fucking problem."

Peterson told *Awful Announcing* that he expects his story—and maybe that of Bishop Sycamore—to continue, and floated the idea of revitalizing the program as a prep school. "And that may be the direction we decide to go with, if we decide to continue it," said Peterson, who acknowledged the numerous challenges Bishop Sycamore could face in the wake of events these last few years. "It's funny, because I still get messages on Twitter from kids who, if we were functioning now, they would come here."

On September 3, 2022, the official Bishop Sycamore Twitter account posted an animation of a heart monitor—still beating. "Since there was a public crucifixion, there must be a public resurrection," the tweet reads, along with the hashtags "#PHASE1" and "#THERIGHTWAY."

Still in touch with Peterson, Johnson isn't sure what involvement he may have in the program of the future. But he's still contributing his levity and big ideas. "They didn't listen to me, I told them they should name it the Richard M. DeWine High School, but they said that didn't work. I thought it was hysterical. I thought everybody was going to laugh about it. Andre doesn't think it's funny at all."